In the 'joy'
of leadership'.

Elizabeth Jeffries

The HEART OF LEADERSHIP

Influencing by Design

HOW TO INSPIRE, ENCOURAGE AND MOTIVATE PEOPLE TO FOLLOW YOU

ELIZABETH JEFFRIES

KENDALL/HUNT PUBLISHING COMPANY
4050 Westmark Drive   Dubuque, Iowa 52004-1840

Other Books by Elizabeth Jeffries:

**Person to Person: Making Connections with
Others and Yourself**

Revised Printing 1996

ISBN 0-7872-2000-0

Library of Congress Catalog Card Number: 96-75128

Printed in the United States of America

10 9 8 7 6 5 4 3 2 1

With great insight, **The Heart of Leadership** takes people to a new level of understanding the joy and opportunities that come from their gift of leadership. Elizabeth speaks to the mind, the heart and the soul, making this book a powerful read.

    —Shawn Kent, author
    Power Presentations

Elizabeth speaks from the heart and helps people live and lead from the inside out! As you process the leadership ideas in this book, you are destined to succeed.

    —William J. McGrane, CPAE
    Founder, McGrane Self-Esteem Institute
    Author, *Brighten Your Day With Self-Esteem*

I'm reading **The Heart of Leadership** for the third time! It's rejuvenating! Elizabeth authenticates a leadership style nurses can identify with. My values as a person do not need to be compromised in order to accomplish my goals as a leader.

    —Ruth Carrico, RN, MA
    Nurse Coordinator
    University Hospital of Louisville

The Heart of Leadership has a human scale. It relates to leaders as real people, with compassion as well as passion and depth as a person rather than a corporate "being." It's a book for real people who want to be strong leaders. The information is so inspiring, we're ordering 100 copies for our nursing leaders for our conference.

    —Judith Latimer, Executive Director
    Texas Organization of Nurse Executives
    Texas Hospital Association

The Heart of Leadership is concise, practical and easy to read—a great handbook for managers. It enables people to think and raise their awareness level.

    —Suzette Pennington
    Vice President, McFaul & Lyons, Inc.

"Elizabeth Jeffries has captured the vital elements necessary to tap your true potential as a person and as a leader. **THE HEART OF LEADERSHIP: Influencing by Design** will help you maximize these elements so you can build and maintain effective teams so necessary in the competitive 90's."

—Sheila Murray Bethel
Co-founder & Chair, Bethel Leadership Institute
Author: *Making a Difference, 12 Qualities That Make You A Leader*

"In **The Heart of Leadership** Elizabeth effectively ties together the need for a personal mission and a career mission. She challenges her audience to truly approach leadership **from the inside out**. If you enjoy her book, you'll love hearing Elizabeth in person!"

—Steven W. Lanter
President and COO
Lanter Companies

"I'm using **The Heart of Leadership** instead of a traditional leadership textbook for my graduate level nursing leadership course. It provides a much more contemporary leadership model, which enriches, enlightens and is a source of encouragement to the students. They say it's 'user friendly.' It doesn't read like a textbook but is just as effective in content!"

—Donna Nickitas, RN, PhD
Graduate Program Coordinator
Nursing Administration
Hunter College
Bellevue School of Nursing

"**The Heart of Leadership** is so practical you can lift the information from the book right now! I used the empowerment quiz right out of the book and gave it to my managers. They loved it. It's **real** stuff."

—Judy Gimber
Assistant Administrator
Patient Care Services
Schumpert Medical Center

"The book is so well written and beautifully inspiring. I have an order on the way for some extra copies."

—Robert S. Allison, President
Doe-Anderson Advertising Agency

"I've been using **The Heart of Leadership** to address the problem of bringing an interdisciplinary team together to improve cardiac patient care. Unlike most leadership books in the business community, it focuses on **leading from the inside out**. I've seen a 200% improvement in patient care!"

—Kathy Sadler, RN
Consultant
Genentech

"We gave **THE HEART OF LEADERSHIP: Influencing by Design** to most of our executive staff and middle managers. The feedback was very positive. They said it was practical and clearly gave them some new concepts about leadership. Most of all, it was consistent with our values as an organization, expressing the new role of the successful manager."

—Stephen A. Williams
Executive Vice-President/COO
Alliant Health System

"This book is one of the best books I have read on leadership. The book is written in an unconstrained reading style that is easy to follow. It sends the message that to be a good leader in this changing environment, a person must be able to think in new terms of motivation, team building, empowerment and not in the traditional ways that people use to influence others."

—Joy G. Kerr
Manager of Personnel
C&I Engineering, Inc.

"We have used **THE HEART OF LEADERSHIP: Influencing by Design** as the framework for developing our management team this year. The chapters on vision and mission have been particularly helpful as each person and each department applies your ideas. They have sparked new enthusiasm in our organization."

—Connie Shaw
Vice President, Nursing
Community Health Center of Branch County

Acknowledgment

In preparing this book there are many people to thank whose contributions extend far beyond what words can express. In particular, Mary Rivard and Shawn Kent have been spiritual companions, committed friends, and constant encouragers. Mary Ann Plichta has been an enabler and a source of energy and support.

I would also like to thank a long list of mentors, associates, authors and philosophers who have guided me in my work and whose observations and insights have strengthened this text. In no particular order they include: Abraham Maslow, Frances Hesselbein, Bill Newkirk, Brian Hall, Ph.D., Michael LeBoeuf, Ph.D., Jeff Davidson, Dr. Norman Vincent Peale, Ken Blanchard, Ph.D., Stephen Covey, Ph.D., Michael Maccoby, Peter F. Drucker, Ph.D., Robert Greenleaf, Peter Block, John Kotter, Ph.D., Robert Half, Dr. Kenneth Kovoch, Sheila Murray Bethel, Denny Crum, Ben Exley IV, Larry Wilson, N. Powell Taylor, James Petersdorf, Rodney Wolford, Bill Arnold, Tom Peters, Albert Marabian, Ph.D. and Socrates.

Also, Jan Carlzon, Ron Zemke, Robert Kelley, Ph.D., Robert Taylor, Ph.D., Karl Albrecht, John W. Gardner, Ph.D., Roger E. Herman, Kop Kopmeyer, Stew Leonard, Richard Bolles, Robert Fulghum, Dr. Herbert Kravitz, Julie Boden, Peter Forella, Robert Levering, Mark Eppler, Robert Conklin, Steve Williams, Denis Quinlan, Lydia Young, Roger Ailes, William J. McGrane, Dr. Leonard Zunin, Natalie Zunin, Frederick Buechner, Vivian Buchan, Marilynn Swan and Warren Bennis, Ph.D.

Elizabeth Jeffries

Contents

Exhibits, Charts and Lists

Introduction

Any organization today, whether it is a large multi-national corporation, a non-profit organization or a start-up entrepreneurial company, requires strong, positive leadership to compete successfully. The same can be said for a department or division within an organization—**leadership** is the key to competitive advantage.

We are in an era of ever-increasing global competitiveness and the ability to actively influence your followers is essential. In my work with hundreds of organizations throughout the United States and Canada, I've found that effective leadership is no accident. The men and women who are able to successfully influence followers have a vision, a mission, and the ability to communicate them to those whom they guide.

As I see it, there are only two basic ways to influence others: **by accident** or **by design**. This book is about becoming proficient at *influencing by design*. It is **the heart of leadership**, the core, the root of what true leadership is all about.

The people you guide look to you for behavioral cues and messages as well as formal instruction, direction and coaching. If you do not vigorously expand your level of awareness and recognition of how your attitudes, beliefs, behaviors, activities, and appearance influence your followers, then you run the risk of *influencing by accident*.

Years of careful observation have convinced me that most effective leaders are masters at influencing by design. In my work with inspiring leaders, I have found that effective leadership characteristics can be developed and that, most assuredly, one can learn to be a more effective leader. Whether you lead one person, or 1,000, a small department, or a Fortune 500 corporation, if you are interested in enhancing your skill in the vital area of influencing by design, then you've picked up the right book.

LEADERSHIP: WHO YOU ARE INSIDE

Leadership is who you are on the inside, so much so that you cannot separate your role in the organization from your inner being. As a leader you are on stage every moment of the working day and beyond—the examples you set, the demeanor you maintain, and the very thoughts that you hold, are transmitted to your followers, like it or not. They, in turn, encode these messages based on their perceptions.

Your ability to lead is a direct extension of your personal history and experiences, education and knowledge, values and beliefs, and how you see the world and the people in it. In 1978, one very charismatic individual influenced 900 followers to relocate some 2,000 miles away and establish a colony seemingly rooted in peace, friendship and support. That person was the Reverend Jim Jones and his followers became the unfortunate victims of the Jonestown, Guyana massacre.

For all his external command and control, Jones was suffering on the inside and lacked even basic components of well-being. In retrospect, it's easy to say he was highly disturbed, yet he was a dynamic, compelling ruler to his followers, many of whom left excellent careers and significant material wealth to follow him.

Being a leader is much more than what you do, or what you say. It is who you are as a person. If you haven't squared away issues internally, you will have little chance of being a positive influence on others externally.

I believe that leadership is an art, a serving, a calling. At its best it is simple, elegant and harmonious. It is intuitive and strategic, involving both the heart and the head. Many leaders don't always hear the call, or want to hear it for that matter. Yet if the elements within prompt you to believe that you are a leader or can be a leader, then you need to follow that guidance. There are no accidents in this regard; trusting your inner voice is essential.

While you may not necessarily feel called to be a leader within your organization there are undoubtedly places within your work team and within your life where you can and do exhibit leadership characteristics. Leadership roles are needed in all walks of life—community, church, education, politics and so on.

The question of whether or not you are a leader isn't dependent upon whether you get paid for your leadership. Many of the greatest leaders in history were never paid in monetary units. Nevertheless, I've found that leadership works best when you are able to incorporate who you are into what you get paid for. When you do your "best work" at the position where you spend the most amount of time and from which you derive your income, then a fitting job-person match has been achieved. This in turn leads to greater energy and higher productivity.

LEADERSHIP VERSUS MANAGEMENT

In his book *Servant Leadership*, Robert Greenleaf observed that effective leaders influence others by serving those they lead. "Servant leadership" is biblical and means that if you wish to lead, you are obliged to serve those who would follow, though the followers may not understand your service to them at the time.

Leadership is the process of influence, literally meaning, "to flow from." It is spiritual and emotional, dramatic and passionate! Leadership is vision with a purpose. It is communication and empowerment and self-mastery. It is more than doing the thing right. That's management. Leadership is doing the right thing.

A leader can only exist in the context of having followers. A leader is a people person who looks forward to interacting with followers on a daily and continuing basis. Management, on the other hand, is tasks, budgets, systems and structures. It is performance indicators, organizational charts, and scheduling. While these are crucial aspects of business, management is not the same as leadership. A person can be a competent manager without having any followers. At my seminars and keynote speeches on leadership, I find that it is important to make this distinction between leadership and management because you can be one and not the other.

Usually, an effective leader is also a fairly proficient manager. The converse is not necessarily true. A capable manager may have little leadership ability. A person can also be in a leadership role but not be a leader, or be the "head of . . ." the organization, department or division but not be a leader.

LEADERSHIP IS AN ART

Leadership focuses on people, on human wants and needs, on creating an environment where motivation can occur. To be an effective leader today requires looking at the wants and needs of people in new ways with new perspectives.

Several authors have likened leadership to an art, and I wholeheartedly agree. Art is always based on a specific form. Yet every time it's applied, the outcome is different. One of my friends, Marilynn Swan, is a skilled artist. She designs and makes beautiful porcelain jewelry. She has mastered the art form of working the raw porcelain, firing the pieces in a kiln, painting the delicate earrings and pins, glazing them and so on. Yet, every time she applies her skills to the materials, each finished piece is different.

And so it is with leadership. Every time a leader relates basic leadership ideas to a follower, the outcome is different because each person is different. No two conversations are alike, no two relationships are the same.

This is the essence of influencing by design, where the leader understands the wants and needs of each follower and is able to serve those wants and needs in a manner that appeals to and enlists the support of the follower. Influencing by design is planned and calculated but always offered with sincerity.

Leaders have focused commitment. They make dreams come alive and are able to unite people in support of those dreams. They inspire others by making them feel significant, and by affirming them. Yes, most leaders are **made,** not born, though seldom made as much by others as by themselves. They are individuals who continually re-invent themselves, perhaps on a daily basis, striving for their best and optimal performance.

The positive, effective leaders I've observed have six important qualities. They all:

1. Have a vision—This gives them a focus and gives them direction.
2. Have a sense of mission—a reason for their vision.
3. Communicate the vision and mission—They are able to translate their intentions into reality and sustain it.
4. Place trust in others—They know that trust is the glue which maintains organizational integrity and is the beginning of empowerment.
5. Master self—They work first on knowing themselves and achieving balance. They know that effective self-management is a prerequisite to leading others.
6. Help motivate others—They strive to create an environment where followers motivate themselves, because leaders know that all motivation is self-induced.

By the time you've finished reading this book, I think that you'll agree that influencing by design is a far more effective approach to leadership than any other means. Here is a brief summary of the sections and chapters that follow:

CHAPTER SUMMARIES

Part I, BY DESIGN, NOT BY ACCIDENT, explores four areas. Chapter 1, LEADING IN A CLIMATE OF CHANGE, provides an overview of the challenges that many leaders face today, and which you may be facing in your own situation. These are tough challenges indeed, but take heart—effective leaders and effective organizations achieve outstanding results year after year in the face of significant challenges. Chapter 2, HAVE VISION OR PERISH, expresses a crucial leadership characteristic: The ability to have a vision, articulate it, and harness it as a driving force for positive achievement.

Chapter 3, WHY ARE WE HERE, ANYWAY? will help take you from vision to mission. Many examples abound of effective organizations and individuals who have developed a mission statement which supports their vision and enables others such as employees, customers, and community, to know what they stand for. Chapter 4, MAINTAINING THE LEADERSHIP EDGE, explores many ways to keep sharp and up-to-date and to master specific disciplines.

Part II, SPREADING THE WORD, explores the importance of and techniques for communicating your vision and mission to those whom you influence. Chapter 5, WHAT THEY SEE IS WHAT YOU GET, focuses on how you visually, vocally and verbally impact your followers. Chapter 6, FORMING A COMMON UNION THROUGH ACTIVE LISTENING, continues the examination of how to powerfully influence your followers through active listening, because most people would rather be heard, not told. It also discusses the fine art of questioning.

Part III, LEADING THROUGH EMPOWERMENT, consists of four chapters which explore different aspects of empowerment. Chapter 7, BUILDING TRUST, describes four components for building lasting mutual trust. Chapter 8, REORIENTING YOUR STAFF, presents a wide look at bringing your current staff to a new level of awareness of today's changes. Unless you are just starting a new organization, you are going to be working with an existing staff or team of followers. They are already oriented, and thinking a certain way. If you want to align them with a revitalized vision and mission, they need re-orientation.

Chapter 9 highlights FINDING AND KEEPING WINNERS, certainly a key for the long term success in your organization or company. Not everyone can or need fit into your organization. Winners, in the context of influencing by design, are those people who want to be effective followers. Chapter 10 focuses on DEVELOPING SELF-DIRECTED FOLLOWERS, introducing the vital concept of followership and discussing how to help your followers find their own vision.

In Part IV, ADVANCED TECHNIQUES for influencing by design, we step on to higher ground. Chapter 11, WORKING WITH THE CUSTOMER CONTACT TEAM, stresses the all-important role of the coach. Chapter 12, WORKING WITH PROFESSIONAL AND SUPPORT STAFF discusses the fine points of establishing solid relationships with key staff.

Chapter 13, MAKING CHANGE WORK FOR YOU, highlights how to implement change in the face of ever-present resistance, increase the level of harmony within your organization, and employ the principles of orchestration to be more effective.

To avoid gender problems throughout, I will use third person, plural pronouns, "they," and "their," when practical. Otherwise, I'll alternate the third person singular pronouns, "he," and "his," with, "she," and "her."

Let's begin then, with Part I, "By Design, Not By Accident."

PART 1

BY DESIGN, NOT BY ACCIDENT

The nature of our society and its workforce is changing rapidly. Many people in leadership positions already have witnessed a profound shift in the character, goals, and aspirations of our contemporary workforce and in the very reasons people hold jobs today. As we will explore in Chapter 1, leadership challenges are mounting. Yet some organizations and individuals are able to remain on course achieving satisfactory, if not outstanding, performance year after year.

The common denominator among leaders who maintain consistency in the face of inconsistent business and social environments is that they've learned to master the elements of **influencing by design.** Chapter 1, "Leading in a Climate of Change," offers a broad look at the changes occurring in our society and workforce.

With a staggering number of workers coming from dysfunctional families, declining pools of skilled labor and nebulous attitudes about work itself, any leader has reason to come to the conclusion that many problems are insurmountable. There are organizations, however, that do well year after year. How do they do it? Chapter 2, "Have Vision or Perish," and Chapter 3, "Why Are We Here, Anyway?" provide some insight. Let's explore.

Leading in a
Climate of Change

1

*The first and last task of a leader
is to keep hope alive.*
                    John W. Gardner

Emerging challenges in the 1990s require a new kind of leader, one with a different idea of what power is and how to use it. This person needs to recognize that leadership includes committing to life-long learning, embracing rapid change, and accepting the ideas and input of followers.

We are seeing the flattening of organizational hierarchies, more cross-linkages between divisions and departments, and a more entrepreneurial approach to leadership, even in some of the most established and well-entrenched multinational corporations, such as Ford Motor Company, Apple computers, Johnson & Johnson, and General Electric.

In progressive organizations today the watchman/supervisor is disappearing with no replacement in sight, while a self-directed workforce is emerging.

THE NEW PACE OF CHANGE

It is not enough that dramatic changes have already transformed the organizational landscapes over the last five to ten years: more are coming with the promise of transforming our society and our organizations in ways that few can perceive

3

and of which many are fearful. World population skyrockets along at a net gain of 240,000 people per day (births minus deaths). The half-life of scientific information is eight years and dropping. Futurists say that by 2005 or sooner half of our scientific and technical information will be obsolete every 18 months.

Never has the need for leadership and followership been so great! With rapid global, technological, and social change there is a pronounced need for leaders and their followers to work as a team—a fully functioning productive unit. Workers today need to assume a wider range of responsibilities and roles, and receive cross training to handle different functions. Additional training may be required every several months. Yet, people everywhere resist change; the inborn human response to change is to hold it off, subvert it, resist it and protect ourselves. *What a marvelous time to develop a reputation for being an effective leader in the face of ever-accelerating change, and to recognize that with change, comes opportunity.*

I find that the best companies and the most effective leaders stay on top year after year, despite change and despite obstacles because they operate from a different viewing point. As we'll see in subsequent chapters, they operate out of a vision, then develop a mission to support that vision. They lead on purpose.

CHANGING VALUES

Today's workforce often holds distinctly different values about work and they may not agree with yours **at all.** Michael Maccoby, in *Why Work: Leading the New Generation,* says, "to motivate this new generation of workers, we need new organizations and leadership. To work more effectively, we need to understand ourselves and each other."

Blue- and White-Collar Blues—Many industries, both blue and white collar, are finding the skill levels and values of the work force to be unsatisfactory. In the construction industry, for example, "poor workmanship including irregular masonry, faulty mechanical systems, and leaking roofs are on the rise nationwide because many contractors are unable to find enough qualified workers for their job sites," according to Peter Forella, a Washington, DC, area architect and construction expert who has witnessed many of these problems first-hand.

Forella says that many contractors today are caught in the squeeze between an active construction market and a dwindling supply of qualified construction mechanics. "The underlying problem has nothing to do with the honest intentions of most American contractors," observes Forella, "but rather the declining skills of the construction workforce and the inability of management to cope with this new reality."

White-Collar Challenges—White-collar workers also present leadership challenges. Consider today's college graduates. They stay at their first job for 18 months or less, and feel little loyalty towards the company or their boss, and perhaps with good reason. In the midst of downsizing, streamlining, RIFS and imposed early retirements, the notion of fending for yourself takes on greater importance. It's hard to build teams when would-be team members are **more concerned about their tenure than their team work.**

RESPONDING TO UNCERTAINTY

The "me"-centeredness of workers today is due less to the "me" decade than to a rational approach to employment uncertainty. This attitude is reflected in others besides recent college graduates. Maccoby says today's young Americans, representing the current and next generation in our workforce, want opportunities for self-development and "a chance to solve problems while working cooperatively with co-workers, customers and clients."

"They are frustrated," says Maccoby "by bureaucracy and leaders who do not share their values." To meet the needs of the new generation and "to find replacements for the traditional incentives that will be denied them, new ways to motivate these people are needed."

Today's typical worker also has many more obligations off the job than ever before. Workers cannot afford mentally, emotionally, and physically to immerse themselves into the job role as did workers of former generations. The single working parent, quickly becoming a social norm, can barely make it in to work in the morning. Among females, wage levels continue to trail that of males, while their ability to get children to school and get to their own jobs on time is a minor miracle!

THE CHALLENGE OF CHILD CARE

When Felice Schwartz introduced the notion of creating separate tracks for female corporate executives who chose to rear children, she encountered a fire storm. Her article, appearing in the *Harvard Business Review*, became the subject of controversy and her plan was dubbed by skeptics as the "mommy track."

Controversy and debate aside, the epidemic need for day care in this country is evident. You can't be an effective leader to followers who are concerned about their children, especially if you don't know about their concerns and show no empathy on this crucial topic.

In our organization, Mary Rivard, one of our key staff members, brought her infant son to work with her for several months of his young life. I realized that the smooth functioning of our small company was significantly dependent upon her ability to feel comfortable both doing her job and caring for her newborn. We made it work. My effectiveness as a leader would have been greatly restricted if I were not tuned in to this key employee's needs. And we possibly would have lost a great worker.

THE CHALLENGE OF ETHNIC DIVERSITY

Twenty-five percent of the American population is now Hispanic, Black, Asian or Middle Eastern, *i.e.*, not Caucasian. Demographers indicate that by 2037 or sooner, the White European descendant population of the U.S. will be in the minority, as will their school-aged children by 1995. In California, White students are already a minority, and in New York they represent only 60% of the student population.

Not surprisingly, massive shifts in the composition of the labor force are already evident. The Hudson Institute forecasts that by the year 2000, only 15% of new entrants to the labor force will be "native white males." Women will account for 61% of new entrants, and minorities will account for 29% (with minority women included in this figure). While the labor force annually grew by about 2% since 1970, a 1% annual growth rate is forecast for the 1990s. Employers will be vying for talent among a smaller pool of primarily non-white, or non-male applicants.

Ethnic concentrations were traditionally centered in coastal areas such as San Francisco, Los Angeles, New York, Philadelphia, and Washington, DC, but this trend is rapidly changing. Many Hispanics, the fastest growing population in the U.S., cling strongly to the Spanish language and see it as inseparable from their ethnic and cultural identity. America's two-hundred-year standard of one national language may not withstand the 20th century. While waves of immigrant influx are nothing new to our society, Western European and Eastern European immigrants throughout the 19th and the start of the 20th century were primarily Caucasian. Yet, skin color probably is not the basic difference between previous and emerging workforces. While the "traditional" American (if one exists) reflects on our proud origins, those recently acquiring U.S. citizenship are more focused toward the future, where hope lies.

As the U.S. strives to become a model of a multiracial society, transition pains are bound to occur. Your organization will inevitably share in that transition. In business, a predominantly white male upper management works with a multicultural and multi-ethnic workforce, with each group maintaining its own expectations about working life.

Some political analysts and social observers fear that a multiracial society will be harder to govern and harder to serve. Others believe that a multiracial society is workable and desirable, whereas a *multicultural* society may produce social problems of a new magnitude. Every society, indeed every organization, requires some set of uniform values to function well. Since organizations are but microcosms of a larger society can we not expect mounting challenges to organizational leadership?

THE NEED AND DESIRE TO WORK

The modern work ethic, where both men and women work outside of the home, started during World War II. Rosie went out to work and found that she liked it. When GI Joe returned from the war, the traditional nuclear family flourished throughout the late 1940s and 1950s and the baby boom generation was spawned.

Rosie's desire to work outside the home had taken hold, however, and slowly throughout the 1950s and 1960s this phenomenon emerged as both a significant social trend and the dominant labor trend. By 1985, 50% of all marriages ended in divorce and a nation of single working parents, both men and women, was in full force.

Why does anyone work at all? "Work ties us to a real world that tells us whether our ideas and vision make sense," says Maccoby. "It demands we discipline our talents and master our impulses. It makes us feel needed by providing recognition for our work." Whereas people's lives used to center around their work, now, for most people, work is just one element, albeit a major element, of a diverse array of activities and responsibilities. Obviously work is a livelihood, and it is where we make our money, but it is viewed in a wholly different light today.

Working outside the home today for many parents, whether married or divorced, is both a desirable choice and a compelling necessity. Sometimes, however, we forget that we have an incredibly blessed economy. Even the single parent, with two or three children, who toils long hours, tends to have the standard American variety of consumer goods which most households throughout the world continue to lack.

Armed with more material goods, financed on credit cards, and more uncertain about their economic future than their counterparts of a generation ago, many workers today, your followers, need their jobs and may like their jobs, but are striving to achieve an ever-illusive balance between their wants and desires and their responsibilities and demands on their time.

FROM HOME TO OFFICE

Organizations are composed of people. The challenges that people face in their personal lives are brought to the office each day. According to Dr. Herbert Kravits and Julie Boden, 96% of Americans come from dysfunctional homes, experiencing either divorce, separation, disruptive chemical dependence, psychological disorders or abhorrent social behavior. If this statistic is off by 20 percent or even 50 percent, what does it say about the challenge you face as a leader?

You are striving to *lead people who come to work already armed with attitude problems, mistrust, resentment and cynicism*, added to those problems they develop while on the job. Mark Eppler, a management consultant based in New Albany, Indiana, who has done extensive research on the effect of cynicism on organizations, says, "Cynicism stems from a lack of trust." It can start anywhere, and it feeds on itself.

How can you have trust in others and not be cynical, when you come from a background that encourages cynicism? You grow up in a dysfunctional family, are surrounded by news-paper, magazine and television reporting that says American leadership is on the wane, Congress is ineffective, and we are losing global market share in our major industries. Before being assigned to a department, you learned first-hand how the company often withholds information important to your job or long term employment.

When you do get company news, it is usually last and perhaps distorted. Worse, the company usually doesn't com-municate with employees until decisions are already made—"done deeds"—with no opportunity for employee expression or feedback. One day, the news could be that the company is re-organizing and your job has been terminated.

This is the all-too-typical scenario of workers today, and perhaps one or more of your own followers.

THE PLIGHT OF YOUR FOLLOWERS

Against this backdrop, today you want to encourage in your followers the notion of continual learning and inspiration, offering a sense of fairness while being practical but firm. You need to be willing to practice new styles and encourage follow-ers to take risks. Without such leadership your team, division or organization will stagger and flounder. . . . With it, your followers may find meaning in the workplace and commit themselves to continued performance and self-improvement.

As a leader, you also are charged with the responsibility for acknowledging the plight of your followers, which indeed may be your own plight, too. World-wide economic competi-tion, this week's technology breakthrough, and shifts in de-mand could put your organization on red alert, or out of business.

Change is happening so fast that the typical worker cannot comprehend it. Earlier in this century, you learned a skill or trade, and it served you for a lifetime. Today, that skill may be obsolete in a matter of years, or *months*. Prior to the 1980s, organizations routinely produced 10- and 15-year plans. I don't believe it's practical anymore. Among my clients, producing just a three-year plan has become a very ambitious undertaking.

A LITTLE STABILITY, PLEASE

Still, human organisms strive for stability. Countless studies show that regular sleep and diet lead to a longer life than do erratic patterns. Married couples tend to live longer than singles. Everything in our being cries out for stability, steady pacing, the "known."

The unknown is mysterious, scary, upsetting. I work with one family-owned company that has been the picture of stability for more than 90 years. This is a healthy organization with steady gross income, a loyal work force and effective leadership.

When ownership was changing hands, the founder and president of the company decided to meet with the entire organization and announce that the transition would not affect the jobs of anyone in the organization. Yet, one of the 30-year managers, whose job was assured, said to me, "I'm scared to death." Fear of the unknown in today's work place is a highly disruptive element and an ever-present challenge for those who aspire to leadership.

MAINTAINING THE CONNECTION

Given the dynamics of our society, what makes employees feel reassured? One of the key ingredients to a satisfied job is a top management that helps employees feel as if they are important as individuals. One survey of 7,800 women from a cross section of business and industry conducted by *Working Woman*, found that the key ingredients of a satisfying job, in order of importance included:

1. Interesting and challenging work
2. Management that makes employees feel important as individuals
3. Never being bored at work
4. Management that provides feedback on performance
5. A job where rewards are strongly related to performance
6. Having a management that is good at setting goals
7. A job that provides status
8. A job with opportunities for advancement
9. Having been consistently successful in your jobs
10. Getting along with your boss
11. Having a management that avoids crisis
12. Having a management that assigns reasonable workloads

Considerable discrepancy exists between what managers think employees want, and what employees say that they want. According to a study conducted by Dr. Kenneth Kovoch, associate professor of business administration at George Mason University, "interesting work," "full appreciation of work done," the "feeling of being in on things," and "job security" were rated as the top four job satisfiers by employees.

When managers were surveyed about their perceptions of what made for a satisfying job for their employees they cited, "good pay," "job security," "promotion and growth as most important," and "good working conditions."

Manager Perception of Job Satisfiers	Item	Employee Responses
1	Good Pay	5
2	Job Security	4
3	Promotion & Growth	6
4	Good Working Conditions	7
5	Interesting Work	1
6	Tactful Discipline	10
7	Loyalty to Employees	8
8	Full Appreciation of Work Done	2
9	Help with Personal Problems	9
10	Feeling of Being In on Things	3

Discrepancy between what employees want and what managers think they want is amazing. "Job security" is the only item that makes each party's top four choices. How can managers productively influence by design if they don't know the wants and needs of the people they are leading? The answer is they cannot, and what occurs frequently in far too many organizations is the growing incidence of influencing by accident, not by design.

The leaders ready to take charge in the 1990s need to be masters of influencing by design, using all of the tools and skills at their disposal. There is really no choice.

THE LEADER AS ORCHESTRA CONDUCTOR

The effective leader maintains a personal connection with each follower despite any other changes occurring. The key is getting new followers to express their thoughts, concerns, fears, whatever they feel. When employees know they have a committed listener, their fears and concerns never seem as large.

In many ways, the business leader is like an orchestra conductor. In a performance, a conductor stands at the center point of a half circle. This enables a free flow of communication to and from the orchestra members. Conductors take the talents of skilled independent players and shape them into a unified whole.

A competent conductor influences and guides each musician in each section of the orchestra. From this leadership, a harmonious blend is created and the outcome is a dramatic, unified piece of music. Similarly, a leader in an organization influences, guides and blends the individual talents of his organizational team. It is done so that each team member experiences a sense of contribution and fulfillment while the organization or team moves on harmoniously toward its goals.

Within an orchestra, the individual musicians are skilled artists. They stay in tune with the melody by listening to the music of each other and watching the signals of the conductor. Together they create exquisite harmony. So too, the individual team members in your organization can create positive outcomes together by listening to and communicating with each other under the influence of an effective leader.

The whole point is, of course, that both the conductor and orchestra know that the music they play is for the benefit of the audience. So too, the effective leader and the organizational team are continually aware that they exist to serve customers.

Let's turn now to two elements of leadership that separate marginal leaders from highly effective ones—vision and mission.

Have Vision or Perish

2

Without a vision people perish.
Proverbs

The most important step on the road to influencing by design is to have a vision. The vision is a future focus, and enables the leader to rise above the mediocre and to stay centered on a possible and desirable future state. By definition, a vision is always farther out on the horizon than you can grasp. It is something to strive for. Though it is not here now, it quite possibly is the way things could be.

Many organizations and many leaders establish new directions and strive for new outcomes. Most write them down with numbers and deadlines just like the management books prescribe. Yet, there is a vital aspect to achievement that comes before you establish quantified goals with time lines. A goal is where you are heading. **The question that needs to be asked and the question that effective leaders always ask of themselves before "where are we heading?" is "what are we heading for?"** "What we are heading for" is the vision.

The vision is not synonymous with goal-setting, though after establishing your vision it certainly is necessary to establish specific goals and to formulate a plan to make them a reality. Such goals and plans usually come in the form of questions, *i.e.,* "what will it take to get there?" You can break down tasks by components or by operations, such as marketing, financing, human resources, etc. Among executive staffs these are often called strategic planning sessions. After producing a strategic plan (not the focus of this book) you then communicate it to those charged with the responsibility of making particular parts of it work.

The vision is a dream, an ideal future, a lofty mental picture that engages the spirit! It comes from the heart, not the head. The vision doesn't have to be practical. It can be pious and idealistic.

Let the vision speak from inside you.
Let it possess you.
Let it be an expression of optimism with caution thrown to the wind!

These may not be comfortable thoughts for many. We are a predominantly left-brain thinking society and the presence of right-brain activity may make us uncomfortable. [One of my favorite expressions in my seminars is, "I'm here to comfort the disturbed, but I'm also here to disturb the comfortable."] Right-brain words such as **passionate, dramatic, idealistic and spiritual** are not readily used or expressed in the business world. As emotional beings, however, it is how we connect with each other. Vision, and mission too, are right brain creations. Visions need to be verbalized. You need to articulate and describe the future of what you want to create for your team. Peter Block, in *The Empowered Manager*, says that a vision statement expresses the contribution that you want to make to the organization, not what you'll receive for it. If you are rewarded, or regarded as number one, good for you, but the vision needs to be worth pursuing for its own sake.

Don't be afraid to make the vision simple and direct. It is okay if it sounds like motherhood and apple pie. It is acceptable if it even sounds a little embarrassing. A vision simplifies the world and implies that all things are possible.

BEGIN WITH YOUR CUSTOMERS

Since your customers keep you in business, determining your customers' needs aids your organization's long-term survival. To formulate your vision, begin with them. Your vision might state,

"we act as partners with our customers . . ." or,
"we fulfill every promise, meet every requirement of our customers . . ." or
". . . whatever it takes to please the customer."

Your vision could encompass how you will engage in internal operations, including how you express support, manage conflict or disagreement, and balance team and individual roles. The important point is to incorporate the values and things you hold most dear about human interaction into your vision. If your vision incorporates a willingness to share and make everyone feel valued and respected, imagine its impact on each of your followers.

When followers are given the opportunity to view the whole plan, and then see the part that they play, they are much more willing to contribute. Even if followers don't have a sense of the total vision, they can always support portions of it.

Robert Fulghum, in his book *It Was On Fire When I Laid Down On It*, tells the story of a visitor to a cathedral under construction in France during the 17th century. The visitor asked a mason what he was doing and the mason replied, "I'm making bricks to build the west wall." The visitor asked a glass cutter what he was doing and the glass cutter responded, "I am making the stain glass window for above the altar."

The visitor then asked an old woman with a broom in hand what she was doing. She responded, "I'm helping to build a magnificent cathedral for the glory of God." Though all three were contributing to its manifestation, she was the only one to whom the visitor spoke who grasped the larger vision.

It is to everyone's benefit that all team members share the larger vision. In doing so, each is better directed on more tasks more of the time. Everyone moves toward having the vision become a reality. Your role as leader is to help all of your followers take up their batons and become leaders themselves.

COMMUNICATING THE VISION

"The essence of political skills," says Block, "is building support for your function and projects through dialogue." You need to be comfortable and at ease talking about your vision so that others can keep it in focus. The more you talk about your vision, the more committed to it you will become and the more easily you will command the interest of others.

"Communicate hope, optimism and conviction," says Block. "Use colorful, excited language and create metaphors and picture images to help others see your vision." Depending on the type of program, at my leadership seminars I may literally or figuratively ask audience participants to draw a picture of their vision. I do this for two reasons:

To quickly demonstrate to them that they all have a vision whether or not it has been expressed in concise terms, and

To get them involved in the act of drawing. This stimulates their right brain and helps creativity to flow.

It's exciting to watch and hear their visions crystallize and so humorous and gratifying to watch our corporate leaders release the playful, childlike part of themselves.

BEYOND THE POSSIBLE

My friend Kop Kopmeyer, a prolific author and retired corporate executive once wrote me a note that said, "Go out and do the impossible, the possible has already been done." If you are trying to rally your team to achieve superior performance or to overcome great odds, and they have never done so before, doing what you have always done is likely to produce the same outcomes. Visionary leaders can achieve extraordinary success! Fred Smith took an unprecedented approach to express mail service when he founded Federal Express. Walt Disney's vision of having an innovative family-type recreational park withstood eight years of rejection from bankers and investors as well as relatives and friends.

Lee Iacocca, already renowned as a great manager, displayed great leadership when he assumed the chairmanship of the bankrupt Chrysler Corporation and confronted the challenges of a failing company head on. Through vision, Iacocca was able to rally his troops and enable the company to regain stability and even profitability in one of the most highly-competitive industries in the world, during a rather weak domestic economic period.

In each instance, mere logic may have dictated that there was no chance. In Fred Smith's case, flying packages into Memphis every night, rearranging them and sending them back out that same night seemed sheer folly—until he made it work. To most people, Disney's idea seemed to be only a modest improvement over a family outing or day at the park. He saw things much differently and ultimately was able to treat generations of children to the fantasy of a lifetime.

Lee Iacocca could have retired comfortably with his stock ownership, severance pay and bonuses from Ford Motor Company. Instead, he took an ailing corporate giant and restored it to greatness, and became lionized for his contribution at Chrysler. In many respects he helped prop up a major pillar in the American economy, the U.S. automobile industry.

You might now be thinking, "Okay, I'm a good manager. I think I'm a good leader, but I have never really created a specific vision for my work. I would like to create one. What do I do to create one?" The odds are *you don't have to create a vision.* You simply have to *find one you already have which is unexpressed.* Unfortunately, and all too frequently, people are not encouraged or given the opportunity to articulate and then act upon their vision.

FINDING YOUR VISION

Here is a ten-step sequence to the question, "How do I find my vision?" or, "How do I know my vision is appropriate?"

1. At seminars I ask participants to quit their jobs, mentally.
2. Then, I ask them to go back to that first day as if they were starting again, to close their eyes and to recall what they had hoped to accomplish when they first started. I often play soft music and in a tranquil voice get them to a near-meditation state. Then I ask them to recall:
   —sensations,
   —colors,
   —sounds,
   —feelings,

of what it was like that first day on the job. What did they hope to accomplish, what great focus loomed on the foreseeable horizon? They might have called it a vision, a dream or a plan. Maybe they gave it no name. I ask them:

"What was it that excited you, enchanted you and stirred your imagination that first day?"

It doesn't matter whether you are the head of your own company or in charge of a department. Most people

recall being excited and full of enthusiasm, eagerly looking forward to new possibilities.

3. Try to recall the day and year, and actual time you first
   walked into this environment.

   Who was there?
   What were you thinking at the time?
   What was going on in your life at that time?
   Who were you talking to?
   What did people say to you?
   What was your posture and demeanor?
   What was your facial expression?

   In recreating a vision or creating one for the first time,
   be assured in knowing that you don't have to have all
   the details. It is unlikely that you even know how you
   are going to get there. At this point, that is not important. In 1963, when John F. Kennedy said, "By the end
   of this decade we will have a man on the moon," no one
   knew how we were going to get there. We only knew
   that we would.

   So recall what it felt like that first day on the job, even
   if only pieces of it emerge. Talk about it; make notes. If
   it is helpful, turn on a tape recorder and quickly capture
   your recollection. From this simple exercise which may
   take anywhere from 10 minutes to two hours some or all
   of your initial vision may once again be articulated or a
   new one clarified.

   It's helpful to have someone guide you through this
   experience. They can ask you questions just as I do
   with my seminar participants. I had a friend do this
   for me and recorded it while I was talking. I really got
   into the experience and found a vision I could get
   excited about.

4. Ask yourself—What are the barriers today to following
   that vision? In your determination, what is holding you
   back? Impediments can be real or imaginary. As you
   begin to identify reasons that the vision may have got-
   ten off track, you often begin to see approaches that you

might take this time. Some extenuating circumstances could have been:

—There wasn't enough time.
—There was little support.
—There was no one to talk to.
—It was opposed by one person who could have helped to make it a reality.
—You lost faith that you could do it.

Perhaps factors outside your organization may have caused you to lose the vision:

—Market competition might have heated up.
—Government regulations restricted your plans.
—Consumer demand shifted.
—You met initial resistance you were unable to overcome.

Visions often get side-tracked simply because we get caught up in the events of the day and lose sight of the big picture—the vision that initially propelled us. Eventually, we get caught in crises management, fighting daily fires, and the vision becomes a distant memory.

5. Having reconstructed the early vision, and identified reasons for getting side-tracked, the next step is to assess how valid that vision is for today and what, if anything, needs to be modified.

   How alive is that vision for you now?
   What pieces of it still matter to you?
   What can you do right now to rekindle the vision and keep the dream alive?

6. Now, repaint the picture. Re-articulate your vision based on where you are today. What is the ideal scenario? Remember, don't be afraid that it is idealistic or grandiose. You are not setting goals, you are creating a vision, a chance to step into the world in a way that you haven't done before.

7. Boil it down, and capsulate your vision in one well-crafted paragraph or sentence. For example, as I pro-

ceeded through my vision experience, I knew my vision was "to be a recognized expert in personal and organizational leadership development." As awkward as I felt expressing it at the time, and as much as I fought off the little voice that said, "You'll never do that," I **really saw myself** making a difference in organizations. It was exciting and very humbling. It remains a lofty vision for me today and truly directs where I'm going.

8. Express your vision to someone you trust. As you hear yourself articulate your vision to someone else it becomes more clear for you. **You have to be careful, however, to whom you speak.** Some people will give you such negative feedback that you may not recover. You may find yourself abandoning a wonderful vision. It is important at this stage to share the vision with those who are generally supportive.

9. After verbally expressing it, you may wish to modify it a bit, so write your new version on paper. If you are visual, you may also want to draw it or create a collage representing pieces of it.

10. Post your vision. After you have boiled it down, modified it and kicked it around, when you have the version that you think is final, type it and post it. Remember to keep it simple. Eventually, you will want to share this vision with your followers, but that is the makings of another chapter.

THE COURAGE TO PRESS ON

If you are concerned that no one else will buy into your vision or that others will see it as folly, realize that if everyone immediately accepted your vision and was confident that it would be achieved, it probably isn't much of a vision. If you have a passionate belief in your vision and if the resistance you encounter is overwhelming, don't change your vision; maybe you need to change your organization.

Liz Claiborne worked for 16 years as a clothing designer with the Jonathan Logan Company. The company offered a limited variety of patterns and sizes, definitely not a match with the diverse body types and stylistic desires of the contemporary woman. For about the last five years of her employment with Jonathan Logan, Claiborne kept telling the higher-ups that the market for women's clothing was changing, and that as a company they needed to respond to those changes.

Repeatedly told at Jonathan Logan to not rock the boat, she eventually left and founded her own company. Claiborne's vision was to create a stylish, affordable, and versatile wardrobe that would appeal to the working woman. This occurred near the time women started entering the workforce in large numbers.

Claiborne's challenge was to maintain the courage of her convictions and follow her dream. So she quick-started her own company. She first made sketches, took them to store buyers and shared her vision with them. Slowly but surely, she found people who could share her vision. Before too long, her styles were in demand among store buyers and, more importantly, among female shoppers. The rest, as they say, is history. She had faith in her vision and Liz Claiborne Inc. grew rapidly throughout the 1960s, 1970s, and 1980s to its number-one position in the women's fashions and apparel industry today.

WAVERING IS COMMON GROUND

On occasion, you may find yourself second-guessing your own vision. It is not uncommon to waver. The mark of an effective leader, however, is to minimize those periods of self-doubt. Though you're not the head of your organization or department, you nevertheless may be faced with the challenge of putting your vision into reality. **Every working day hundreds of thousands of people face rejection, and even ridicule, as they envision things the way they can be as opposed to the way they are.** This is where the personal characteristic of courage comes into play. Courage comes from the latin word "cor," meaning heart. A leader committed from the heart can meet these challenges head on.

VISIONS ON ALL LEVELS

You may have a vision for the organization or company, a vision for the department, even a personal vision. You can even have a vision for each of your followers and help them to develop their own visions, as we will discuss in Chapter 10.

Several years ago I started working with Ohio Valley-Clarksburg, Inc. I was leading a strategic planning session with the senior managers when the company's president, Ben Exley IV, expressed his vision to the executive staff. When he told them of the fantastic growth that he foresaw, many people nearly fell off their chairs! No one was prepared for his majestic dream—he had never expressed it in those terms before. He spoke of the number of employees they would have, places where they would be selling, the kind of business they would develop, the market share they would enjoy and so on.

As he spoke about his vision he got very excited and the listeners caught that excitement. Though initially stunned, many left the meeting super-charged believing that the vision might one day become a reality. Today most of what was articulated that day has come to pass, though in different ways.

Suppose that you are not the president of the company; you run a department. Envision what your department would look like in its ideal state:

- What level of service would you be providing?
- What type of interaction would team members have with each other?
- How would you be perceived in the marketplace?.
- What type of new employees would you be attracting?

I introduced this exercise to a group of nursing managers in a seminar. Most agreed that a highly worthwhile vision would be to have all the people in their department recognize that the patient was really the customer, and ideally all activities focus on improving treatment of the customer and the customer's perception of the nursing department and the hospital. Further, they decided that the vision included instilling in all team members the notion and reality that it is the customer who is signing their pay checks.

Next, I asked these managers what they were willing to do to make this vision a reality. One manager responded that she would teach her people, one step at a time, until everyone knew and understood. She realized she would have to continually be talking about this vision, getting others to talk about it, and making it a part of her everyday consciousness. She knew that living out her vision doesn't just happen. It is a journey. It may even be a life-long journey.

COLONEL SANDERS HAD VISION

Everyone undoubtedly has eaten at a Kentucky Fried Chicken restaurant at one time or another. Few people realize, however, that Harlan Sanders, known as Colonel Sanders, founded the company at age 66 following 17 years of experimentation and rejection. Fried chicken had long been one of the Colonel's staples at the Sanders Cafe in the mid 1930s. The problem with fried chicken was that pan-frying was slow, and deep fat-frying was unsuitable for the Colonel's precise standards.

In 1939, Sanders used a pressure cooker for the first time to discover an ideal method for cooking the type of chicken he wanted to offer. With the pressure cooker he was able to cook chicken that retained full favor and moisture.

Over the next two decades he continued to perfect his recipe for chicken and in 1953 sought to establish a franchise business. His technique was to drive up to restaurants, and offer to cook a piece of chicken for the manager and employees. If they liked it, he would stay on for several days and cook chicken for customers. If customers liked it, there was an informal agreement with the owners.

Life on the road was tough for the now 65-year-old traveler. After two grueling years on the road he had only collected a total of five franchises while experiencing rejection at hundreds of restaurants. The Colonel had a vision, however, that one day his chicken would be served across America. He stuck with his plan and between 1955 and 1960 signed up more than 200 outlets. By this time, at the age of 70, he left the road, and allowed franchise inquirers to come to him.

John Y. Brown, Jr., a highly successful Kentucky businessman, sensed that "Kentucky Fried Chicken" had a tremendous potential and in 1964 bought the company from Colonel Sanders for $2 million plus a guarantee to pay the Colonel a lifetime annual salary of $40,000, subsequently raised to $75,000 a year. Colonel Sanders remained on the Board of Directors through 1970, at that time, a robust 80 years old.

In all, the Colonel suffered more than 900 rejections but as a visionary leader he understood that it is not the rejections that count, **it is the acceptances.** Without the Colonel's vision for having this recipe sell and having people enjoy it, Kentucky Fried Chicken as we know it simply would not exist.

REVITALIZING YOUR VISION

A vision only works if it is kept alive. Leaders skilled in influencing by design use any opportunity in which to do so. How often do you need to re-examine your vision, perhaps reword it, and rededicate yourself to it? There are no clear answers. For many organizations it is once annually, usually at the start of the fiscal year or new year. Some organizations choose to do it on the anniversary of their inception or during their annual retreat. It doesn't have to be annually however. Any time there is a significant event, a breakthrough, or even a challenge, is a good time to re-articulate the vision.

REVEREND HESBURGH'S VISION FOR NOTRE DAME

The Reverend Theodore Hesburgh retired in May, 1989 as the President of The University of Notre Dame, following 35 years of service and what some regarded as one of the most distinguished reigns of any major U.S. university president. Interviewed just after stepping down, he noted that when he first came to South Bend, he had a vision that Notre Dame could become the most prominent Catholic college in America. Then, for three-and-a-half decades Hesburgh nurtured, communicated, and lived that vision.

In 35 years, enrollment nearly doubled to 9,670 students. Back in 1952, 30% of the incoming class were rated in the top 10% of their high school classes. By the time Hesburgh left, it was 95%. The university's endowment increased from $9 million to $400 million plus and its yearly budget from $9.7 million to $176.6 million. The university has developed top-rated departments in philosophy, theology and mathematics, and made other notable achievements:

- A new 14-story library containing 1.6 million publications opened the month of his departure.
- Campus buildings increased from 48 to 88, and counting.
- Trustees now include men and women, Black, Whites, Hispanics, Protestant and Jewish members from all over the U.S. and other countries.
- Formerly an all-male school, in 1972 the university went coed, and today has a 33% female population.
- Since 1962, 95% of Notre Dame's football players have graduated, compared with far lower figures at other major universities, generally averaging between 20 and 50%.

Why was Hesburgh able to achieve such outstanding results? One of his long-time associates said that Hesburgh was "playing by another set of rules." He continually communicated his vision to the department heads, deans, trustees, alumni and the students themselves. He approached his work with enormous energy and focus, travelling some 150,000 miles a year speaking on behalf of the university.

During the campus unrest of the 1960s, Hesburgh was confronted with protesting students. He delivered a message that the students would be given 15 minutes "to decide whether to desist or be suspended." While none of the students was happy with such a choice, most complied and as a result Notre Dame experienced relative calm that most other colleges were not able to achieve.

His followers observed that his faith keeps him strong. All during his reign at Notre Dame and since then, he stayed true to his personal beliefs and commitments. Quoted in *Time* magazine, upon retiring Hesburgh said, "The very essence of leadership is you have to have a vision. It has to be a vision you articulate clearly and forcefully on every occasion. You can't blow an uncertain trumpet."

Why Are We
Here, Anyway?   **3**

*We are not just managing for the
sake of being great managers. We
are managing for the mission.*
                    Frances Hesselbein

W*hy do you get up in the morning?*
Have you ever stopped and asked yourself why you get up
in the morning? It may seem a simplistic exercise but try it
some morning. Many would-be leaders get up in the morning
with no sense of where they are headed and understandably
convey the same to their followers.

Is the energy level of your staff decreasing? Do they seem
less and less attentive? How can you influence by design when
you don't know why you are coming into work that day, or
worse, why you come to work at all? It can't simply be to show
up, put in the hours, accomplish a few things and draw a
paycheck.

Dr. Norman Vincent Peale says, "everyone of us is born by
Almighty God for a purpose, and the fact that we are still here
indicates that we have not achieved that purpose completely,
otherwise we would no longer be here." There is no avoiding it.

To be an effective leader, you have to deal with some personal issues on a philosophical level.

I believe that most leaders really want to make a difference.
They clearly define who they are and what they want to contribute to the world, to their organization, and to their staffs.

Many have a deeply-sensed internal need not only to make a difference but to leave something of themselves in our society before they depart. Making a difference, of course, is seldom easy. Successful organizations and individuals use mission statements to aid them in their quest to make a difference.

IN SUPPORT OF YOUR VISION

Your vision, any vision, is best supported by a mission, often expressed as a statement. A mission statement is a general description of why an organization, team or individual exists. Like the vision, it is based on passion, forward thinking and service. The difference is that the mission statement serves as an expression of a vision. A mission statement usually involves making an impact in some way. The mission statement expresses your vision in terms that others can easily understand and follow. It can be composed of high-minded language or simple terminology.

Mother Teresa feels that the greatest disease of human kind today is not cancer, heart disease or tuberculosis, but the feeling of being unwanted and uncared for and deserted by others. "The greatest evil is the lack of love and charity," she says.

Her *vision* is to have the poor live happy, productive lives.

Her *mission* is to care for the poor and help them to be better off.

She once expressed her mission as, "doing small things with great love." Her message is clear, simple and direct.

A mission is the destiny or chosen end of your efforts. It can also be regarded as the service on which a person is sent or as a calling on the part of individual, company or organization. When you are on a mission, you are sent or directed with authority to perform a definite task.

MISSION VERSUS VISION

One way to look at the difference between vision and mission is that vision is how you would like something to be, and your mission statement reflects why you chose that vision. A mission statement can be seen as a standard, what you expect to achieve, whereas vision can look beyond the mission. Mission tends to be more stationary; vision tends to be more dynamic.

With vision you ask questions such as, "Where do we want to go next?" and "What would we like to do?" The mission statement is the ship, the vision is the horizon. *The tricky thing about vision and mission is that while the vision is created first and is supported by the mission, as an organization lives its mission, it needs to continually redefine its vision.* In this sense, the two exchange places in chronology.

The mission statement can have the feeling of a vision but is not quite the same. It could also be a statement of what exists, *i.e.,* "We are in the business of producing . . ." but need not be limited to such language. A mission statement tends to be general rather than specific. It is the global reason for being, the reason you are in existence.

MISSION IS SPIRITUAL

Think of vision as being a right-brain activity. A vision springs forth; you don't know why but you feel it pulling you in its direction. With mission, you then step back and analytically consider the vision you have chosen. Ask yourself what is the underlying reason (your mission) you chose that vision.

Was it to serve humanity?
Was it to provide excellent customer service, or
To treat your employees fairly?

To make a contribution to society?
Or is it all of the above and more?

The mission statement may require several paragraphs to fully articulate. That's okay, the bigger your vision, the more complex your mission statement may be. The mission can also address making a superior product or generating substantial prosperity and includes "why" you want to do that.

A LEADERSHIP TOOL

A mission statement, while of value to all who interact with the organization, specifically serves leaders of the organization because it offers an expression of their vision and sense of stewardship. Stewardship is the moral responsibility for the careful use of time, money, talents or other resources, especially with respect to the principles or needs of an organization. A well-crafted mission statement embodies the core of the values of the organization. It creates the context, gives meaning, direction and coherence to everything else.

The best mission statements are simple, generic and general. They can include such elements as acceptance, love, growth, contribution, opportunity and balance. They often make reference to all stake holders in the organization.

USING THE MISSION STATEMENT
TO INFLUENCE BY DESIGN

When attempting to establish a mission for your organization or team, much the same process as formulating a vision is followed, with some notable exceptions:

- Make it simple, clear, direct and possible. Whereas the vision need not be or seem possible, the mission statement most definitely describes something concrete and attainable.
- Define who you are within the statement, *i.e.*, dedicated professionals, a service-oriented company, an organization committed to . . . This isn't necessary for your vision, but it is for the mission.
- Articulate your purpose. What are you striving for, what goals or objectives do you hope to achieve, what level of service do you wish to offer, what kind of environment do you want for your employees?

ON A MISSION FOR THE GIRL SCOUTS

In 1976 Frances Hesselbein became the executive director of the Girl Scouts of America, the largest nonprofit organization in the free world. The proud tradition of Girl Scouts was on the wane, however, and membership was dropping. Some 300 different councils governed the organization with no clear mission.

In many ways the Scouts had lost touch with the interests of young girls. With more mothers working, fewer mothers were interested in becoming troop leaders. It seemed as if the organization were more suited for an earlier era. Hesselbein, however, was on a mission to restore the important role GSA could play in the lives of millions of young women.

Hesselbein revamped the organization chart and made it circular, united the hundreds of councils, initiated management training programs, and perhaps most important, employed marketing research to determine social changes and emerging areas of interest for potential members.

Over the last decade and a half, the proud tradition and membership roles of the Girl Scouts of America have been restored.

GIRL SCOUTS OF THE UNITED STATES OF AMERICA: PURPOSE OF MOVEMENT

. . . do dedicate ourselves to the purpose of inspiring girls with the highest ideals of character, conduct, patriotism and service that they may become happy and resourceful citizens.

OTHER STERLING EXAMPLES

Below are other examples of mission statements, although not every organization terms them as such. For example in the case of Doe-Anderson they call their mission statement, "The Way We Do Business." Colgate U.S. calls their mission, "Our commitment . . ." Ohio Valley-Clarksburg Inc. calls it, "Our Mission." National City Bank of Louisville, Kentucky, uses the term, "Our Philosophy." Domino's Pizza Distribution Corporation uses the term "Mission Statement."

At Winona Memorial Hospital in Indianapolis, now known as Midwest Medical Center, a card is given to all employees called, "Our common mission," and a large banner containing a huge version of the Winona Hospital mission, signed by 600 employees, graces the wall in the reception area where visitors first enter. That is a sense of mission and commitment. At Colgate U.S.'s New Albany, Indiana, plant the mission is also printed on a banner and it is hung over the top of the door just inside so everyone sees it as they enter. It, too, is signed by hundreds of employees and top-level managers. Colgate U.S. distributes a small laminated card that all employees can carry with them in their wallets.

Here are some examples of mission statements. Most of them are from our client organizations.

Doe-Anderson Advertising Agency— Louisville, Kentucky

The Way We Do Business at Doe-Anderson

We will work to make Doe-Anderson a valuable partner to our clients as a result of the business ideas and services we provide.

We will never give a client less than our very best thinking and service. Size is not an excuse. Nor is budget. Nor is time.

We will spend our clients' resources as if we were spending our very own. We will search for ways to get the same for less, or more for the same.

We will not go after any new business with anything less than a driving obsession to get it.

We will not retain an account we don't service with the same drive and enthusiasm it takes to get a new client.

We will strive to do all work on time, on target, on budget.

Winona Memorial Hospital, Indianapolis, Indiana

Our Common Mission

We are Winona Memorial Hospital, a proud team of individuals providing healthcare that merits the confidence of those we serve and which is unique in its compassion. This compassion lives within us.

In partnership with our Medical Staff, we meet the physical, emotional and personal needs of our patients, their families and our community.

In partnership with one another, we provide an atmosphere of trust and respect which challenges each of us to reach our full potential both personally and professionally.

Through excellence in all we do, we realize a profit that enables us to provide innovative healthcare services now and to reinvest in the future.

Colgate U.S., New York, New York

Mission

Colgate-Palmolive Company is a leader in providing consumer products and services that meet or exceed the needs and expectations of consumers worldwide. Our mission is to improve continuously our products and services so that our Company, our people, our business partners and our shareholders will grow and prosper, enabling us to become the best global consumer products company.

Values

Our Company embraces the following values as the essence of our success:

People: Colgate people are our most important resource, and they determine our corporate knowledge, energy, and creativity. We recognize and respect the diversity, strength, ingenuity and imagination of every individual.

Products: Colgate products should be the best at delighting the consumer in quality and value. Our products are the ultimate result of our efforts, and they determine our reputation.

Profits: Profits are necessary to ensure our existence, growth, and a reasonable return to our shareholders, the owners of our business.

Federal Express, Memphis, Tennessee

Federal Express is committed to our PEOPLE—SERVICE—PROFIT philosophy. We will produce outstanding financial returns by providing totally reliable, competitively superior global air-ground transportation of high priority goods and documents that require rapid, time certain delivery. Equally important, positive control of each package will be maintained utilizing real time electronic tracking and tracing systems. A complete record of each shipment and delivery will be presented with our request for payment. We will be helpful, courteous and professional to each other and the public. We will strive to have a satisfied customer at the end of each transaction.

Ohio Valley-Clarksburg, Inc., Wheeling, West Virginia

. . . Our Mission . . .

We are . . .

A Leading Team of Distribution Specialists.

We Provide . . .

Quality Health Care Services and Products to Pharmacies.

We Are Committed To . . .

Anticipating and Fulfilling Our Customers' Needs In Order To Enhance Their Success.
Creating An Atmosphere For Our Employees That Encourages Their Personal and Professional Development.
Maintaining A Solid Financial Base For Continued Growth and Stability.
Integrity In All Interactions With Those We Serve.

National City Bank, Louisville, Kentucky

Our Philosophy

We will deliver a level of banking that distinguishes us in this marketplace. Within the limits of honesty and fairness, we will work as a team to:

- Stress caring and an atmosphere of fun in all areas where employees interact with customers and each other.
- Constantly improve our skills and knowledge in order to deliver the best service and products that our customers require.
- Actively and aggressively extend relationships with current customers and pursue new customers and opportunities.

Our dynamic involvement must create the feeling that no bank will work harder than we will to serve our customers.

The Domino's Pizza Distribution Corp., Ann Arbor, Michigan

"Mission Possible"

Through continuous innovation and living the Golden Rule, we will attain:

- Customer's belief that we are the best place to shop for their needs
- Team members who can't think of a better company to work for
- Community (government) that considers us a fine example of what business should be
- Parent company proud to have us as part of their team
- Suppliers excited enough to call us their favorite account

These result in constant improvement in those key operational areas so vital to our success.

Hospital Corporation of America, Nashville, Tennessee

HCA, Quality Framework Policy

Our Mission Is:

To attain international leadership in the healthcare field

To provide excellence in healthcare

To improve the standards of healthcare in communities in which we operate

To provide superior facilities and needed services to enable physicians to best serve the needs of their patients

To generate measurable benefits for:

- the Company
- the Medical Staff
- the Employee
- the Investor
- and, most importantly, the Patient

Quality Definition

At HCA, achieving quality means the continuous improvement of services to meet the needs and expectations of the patients, the physicians, the payers, the employees, and the communities we serve.

At Jeffries & Associates our mission is, "to empower people and teach them how to create an environment that increases productivity and profitability in the organization, more effectively serve their customers, and gain a deeper sense of personal fulfillment from their work."

We go on to describe who we serve: "people with a desire to expand their personal potential, who want to do their best work, obtain a deeper sense of contribution to those they serve and live a high self-esteem life style." At the organization level this includes organizations aspiring to new levels of growth, that want to create or expand a culture based on values of integrity, service and commitment to all stake holders.

Creating our mission statement helped us to hone in on who we are and served to make our work more meaningful.

LEADERS WITHOUT A MISSION

Often some leaders cannot influence by design and incur substantial people problems because they themselves are the root of the problem. They don't create a vision, or if they do they are not able to articulate the vision to others. They don't create a mission statement which serves as the rock and foundation by which the organization or department operates.

If staff has a problem with "motivation," chances are they may be having a problem with management. I had a client who wanted me to come in and "motivate" his staff. During my preliminary research before presenting an implementation plan, I found that everyone I spoke to was in complete agreement: The client—the person who called me in—was the source of the problem. Both employees and customers offered fairly similar observations about his lack of ability as a leader. As I further examined the situation, I found that the key ingredient he was missing was the ability to effectively communicate his vision and sense of mission.

MISSION ON THE DEPARTMENT OR TEAM LEVEL

A well-crafted mission statement gives your followers a sense of "being able," of having a reason for being and a capability to be it. The Roman philosopher Virgil said, "They are able because they think they are able." If you operate a department or have but a handful of followers, you nevertheless could create a one-page sheet that would define your mission. You could circulate it to your followers so that it immediately becomes of service.

Throughout your career and various leadership posts, you have many options for creating key statements which guide your actions and those of your followers. In other words, you have no excuses for not working on your mission statement today.

THE MISSION STATEMENT IS CREATED AS A TEAM

Ideally, the mission statement is created by a team, whereas the vision statement is often created alone. Get your team together in an atmosphere of no disturbances, and ask them some penetrating fundamental questions. At Jeffries & Associates, we take a weekend every year to ask ourselves:

"Why are we here?"
"Why do we come to work every day?"
"What do we want to do and be as an organization?"

These questions lead to many other questions, such as:

"Who is it we serve?"
"How come we chose that particular market?"
"What do we believe about our customers and their needs?"
"What in me/us will be fulfilled by serving the customer?"
"What is my/our uniqueness?"

Mary Rivard, our marketing director, began to explore why she has stayed with our company for over six years. She found that she stays because her personal mission is in alignment with our company mission. She believes in me, and she believes in what we do. Working at Jeffries & Associates provides her the opportunity to live her values through her work.

When I interview new job candidates, I attempt to understand if they have a mission and why specifically do they want to work here. Candidates with no sense of purpose or one that is not in alignment with ours, as a rule, simply don't work out. (More on "Finding and Keeping Winners" in Chapter 9.)

IT'S NOT ALWAYS COMFORTABLE

If we only did what we felt was comfortable or practical the work of the world would never be accomplished. I have been telling a story in my seminars for years that gets at the core of what leadership and mission is all about. The story is about Jonah, the biblical character who was swallowed by a whale.

Jonah was asked by God to go to Nineveh and preach. You can almost hear Jonah saying, "Who me? You have to be kidding. No thanks, I don't think I am the person for the job. No one is going to listen to me. I don't really know what to say. Besides it's so far to go! I do appreciate your considering me, but I really think you have the wrong person."

To ensure that he is not selected for this assignment Jonah hops aboard the first passing ship and sails off, hoping that God will eventually choose someone else for the assignment.

After setting sail, the ship heads into a big storm. Jonah takes it personally, feeling that God is trying to punish him for not accepting the Nineveh post. Rather than have everyone on the ship incur God's wrath, Jonah jumps overboard.

Eventually, he is swallowed up by a whale and for three days Jonah sits in silence in its belly. During this time, he considers his life and all that has transpired. Inside the whale it's very dark—Jonah cannot even see his hand in front of his face. It's also damp and smelly. It's also lonely—there's no one to talk to. Jonah wants out! He begins to think that any place else is better than being here, even preaching at Nineveh.

Lo and behold, God in his mercy has the whale cough Jonah up onto the shore. You can almost see Jonah standing there on the shore saying, "Okay, God you win! I'll go and preach at Nineveh!"

I didn't realize until a few years ago that psychologist Dr. Abraham Maslow coined the phrase the "Jonah Complex" to describe a documented, psychological group of symptoms found in people who run away from their real mission in life. Jonah's story demonstrates, as Dr. Abraham Maslow concluded, that you can't run away from your greatness. You cannot run away on this earth from what you are really here to accomplish. The Jonah Complex, as Maslow describes it, is that tendency within each of us to try to run away from our greatness, to not accept the challenge we feel calling from within us.

We've all had times when we felt like Jonah, when we felt we were in the whale's belly. It's almost a common human reaction to conclude, "I am really not the one, I'm not up for this, I don't even know why I am having these thoughts." We are great rationalizers when we want to be—particularly when we want to avoid recognizing our calling. That's why I said in the introduction to this book that we often don't want to hear the call of leadership.

I believe we are all here for a reason, though we may have different jobs to do. We are each given different talents and gifts, and we become stewards of these talents and gifts. We are charged with the responsibility of making the most of them and using them to create good.

YOUR MISSION HAS A SPIRITUAL QUALITY

On that final judgment day, I believe that we will be asked not what we did but whether we used the talents and gifts that we had been given.

The question facing most would-be leaders is, "How do I know what I am supposed to do?" Often, the answer doesn't come easy. Richard Bolles in *What Color is My Parachute* says, "You will never know your career mission without having an understanding of your personal mission. The two are inextricably linked."

He says that our mission here on earth is one which we share with the rest of the human race. That is, to do what we can, moment by moment, day by day, to make the world a better place—following the guidance from within and the needs around us.

There is a mission that is uniquely yours and no one else can have it simply because they are not you! It is:

- to exercise the Talent which you came here to use—your greatest gift which you most love to use
- in the place or environment which most appeals to you
- for the purposes that are most apparent in the world

Frederick Buechner in *Wishful Thinking—A Theological ABC* says, "There are all different kinds of voices calling you to all different kinds of work, and the problem is to find out which is the voice of God rather than that of society, say, or the super ego, or self-interest . . . the place God calls you to is the place where your deep gladness and the world's deep hunger meet."

Richard Bolles believes that your personal mission is spiritual and you can't deal with your career mission without understanding the spiritual aspects of it. I realize that is not a comfortable view for most people. It is often uncomfortable even for people who understand their mission to express it to others.

Stephen Covey in *Seven Habits of Highly Effective People* says that until you can stand in front of others and talk about your mission in life you can't hope to be an effective leader. I find his words inspiring. They helped me to crystallize my perception that we are not here to just take up space—I'm not and neither are you. As long as we are still here, each day represents a new opportunity to head in the direction of our greatness.

Every person and every company has a reason for being here and has a story behind them. Until we are aware of and understand those stories, we can't hope to be effective leaders. Until we deal with those stories, until we deal with people on an intimate level, we are never going to be able to help them find and fulfill their missions.

What would it take for you to begin—or to revitalize—your organization's mission? Would you be willing to gather your key staff and find out in their own words their view of why the organization/team exists? Are you up for the challenge of determining how their personal missions fit in with the organization mission?

Maintaining the Leadership Edge

4

*We expect our leaders to be better
than we are . . . and they should
be, or why are we following them.*
Paul Harvey

Leaders who have proven to be effective over the long haul share some common characteristics and capabilities. One is the ability to lead in a climate of change, as we discussed in the first chapter. Another is leading by example, the subject of Chapter 5, and another is the ability to be an active listener, presented in Chapter 6.

In this chapter, we'll focus on critical elements that help maintain the leadership edge, including: the leader as scholar, the importance of high self-esteem, releasing the child within, mastering speaking skills and achieving balance.

THE LEADER AS SCHOLAR

Leaders know that they need to be life-long learners— school is never out. There is never one way, one system, one formula for doing something that is the end all and be all.

When I graduated from eighth grade, I remember being excited and telling my father how great it felt to get to commencement, the end, as I said then. Looking at me with a smile, Dad got out the dictionary and we looked up the word "commencement," which of course means the beginning. In our society, where technical knowledge is rapidly and continuously being replaced, can any leader, at any time, rest on what he currently knows, or the way he currently does things?

Even if change and technical knowledge weren't coming so fast, as time marches on, an effective leader would still need to be a lifelong scholar to stay ahead of the pack, to learn new ways of interacting with people, and to re-form the vision as necessary.

The definition of a scholar is someone with a specific body of knowledge. Or someone who is skilled in a specific area.

What is the last book that you read that contributed to your development? It need not be on leadership or management. Many leaders learn well from the classical literature, poetry, and philosophy. If you saw the movie, **"Dead Poets' Society,"** you got a vivid reminder of how much we can learn from literature: "Carpe diem,"—seize the day. From *Gulliver's Travels*, and *Don Quixote*, to *Riders of the Purple Sage*, wisdom has lingered on for centuries.

Increasing General Awareness—To "up" your leadership skills and to be more effective at influencing by design, may I suggest that you vigorously pursue avenues that increase your level of awareness, understanding of human relations, and knowledge of our society or our planet. I know many effective leaders who are always clipping articles from newspapers and magazines. They are looking for the next trend or leadership principle that they can bring back to the job and apply. They are opportunity-oriented. Many spend a substantial amount of time growing in a particular area of interest. Let me explain further.

When confronted with all the things that you need to know in today's society, it is easy to feel overwhelmed. Why not, as some leaders do, totally immerse yourself for three or six months in, say, learning a new computer software program? Or learning a language? Or the latest in neurolinguistic programming?

With friends and colleagues, I often make year-long commitments to learn all I can about a particular body of knowledge. One year it was meditation, another year, organizational dynamics. Still another year, it was interpersonal communications.

Recently, I have been interested in self-esteem, an important topic for individuals and for our society as a whole. As you raise your level of self-esteem, you are more effective in dealing with the people around you, and in making society work. My goal related to self-esteem is to understand it better, apply it more effectively, and more fully incorporate it into my everyday life.

For you, this could be the year you choose to get further into the technical aspects of the job. Or, this could be the year you learn all you can about handling rapid change. Take some two- and three-day seminars. Grab a few good books, cassettes and videos on the topic. Make it a topic of conversation with your followers, peers and family. Have your mental perceptors tuned to clipping out items related to your topic.

After a year or less of concentration on a particular topic you'll find that you quickly move to mastery. It frequently takes less effort than we first suspected to become well-educated or have a sense of mastery of many areas of interest.

Which Topic?—How do you know which topic to focus on? The answer is, "What are your needs right now? What excites you? What seems to be tugging at you gently?" One of my clients has spent the last six months becoming more at ease with standard office equipment. He decided he would not let fax, modems, laser printers, and hard disks scare him anymore. He read about them, experimented with them, and even retained subject matter consultants to give him spot assistance.

After a few months, he concluded that these office support items are not scary, they are friends that help him to make money. He is far more proficient with this equipment now and looks forward to expanding and upgrading his office equipment in the near future.

Do you feel overwhelmed by your responsibilities? Or, is there little time to learn all the things you would like and need to learn? Then pick one topic, for three months or so, and give it the benefit of your extracurricular concentration. If you attempt to learn eight new things at once, you are bound not to learn any of them well. You don't have to be perfect before moving on to the next area of learning. Your goal is to gain some sense of mastery, to be able to discuss it, apply it and teach it to others. Teaching your new learning, by the way, is the step that grounds you in mastery of a topic.

A Continuing Investment—Being a scholar requires making an investment in time, energy and money. You can resist, you can say you don't have the time, energy, or money. Yet it is a non-negotiable proposition. To be a leader requires being a scholar.

To be a scholar requires initiative. Your company may not always pay for your educational pursuits. Don't wait for the company to pay for them. Take them on as your personal responsibility. That $300 that you pay for the seminar or $22.95 for the book is going to be returned to you many times. You are making a long term investment in yourself and your ability to effectively influence others. I know many would-be leaders who will not shell out dollar one, *i.e.*, "the company should pay for it." It's your career, your effectiveness, and your life each day.

Members of a professional group I belong to, who shall remain nameless, are fussing over the cost of an annual newsletter that they currently receive which strongly supports their career and income efforts. Some people say the newsletter should be free. Others think it would be a bargain at twice the five dollar price.

Life to me is like a poker game. Before you can play the game you have to ante up. Most people are not willing to ante up in life. Some think they are entitled to play the game first, then put something in. Yet life works the other way around. I gladly pay the five dollars per newsletter issue because I always get at least one idea that may save me a couple thousand dollars in misdirected efforts, or helps me to be more prosperous in some way.

Too many would-be leaders don't see the correlation between the dollars you may need to spend to keep yourself educated and the long-term results. The unwritten law of the universe is that you have to put something out before the returns will come.

LIVING A HIGH SELF-ESTEEM LIFESTYLE

Self-esteem is the way you feel about yourself. It is that deep down feeling that says, "I am a worthy person." The high self-esteem individual doesn't compare himself to others or measure his self-worth by his net worth. He is able to value both himself and other people.

You can't give away what you don't have. If you don't feel good about yourself, you are not going to feel good about other people or treat them well. The key to self-esteem is accepting yourself just as you are, right now. You don't have to do, say or work on anything. Just for being, for merely existing, you acknowledge yourself as a worthy person. This doesn't mean you aren't pro-active in growing. It just means you have choices.

Self-esteem is a gift that you give yourself. If you have not given it to yourself lately, offer it today. Here are some personal affirmations you can make on the road to maintaining high self-esteem:

- I accept myself as I am right now.
- I choose to feel worthy and complete.
- I easily accept myself and others.
- I am a competent, capable person.
- I am at peace with myself and the world.

In the workplace it's easy to spot the high self-esteem leader. For one, followers know it and feel it. The high self-esteem leader makes each of his followers feel better about themselves. Conversely, the low self-esteem leader is not happy with himself, and generally not happy with others. He may demoralize his staff, and manage based on his moods. The low self-esteem leader, if indeed such terms can be presented together, engages in considerable negative self-talk.

The Perils of Negative Self-Talk—Everyone engages in negative self-talk on occasion. High self-esteem individuals recognize how costly, even damaging, negative self-talk can be. They often check themselves when they recognize they are engaging in it. The low self-esteem individual subjects himself to a constant stream of negative self-talk ranging from why he is not making a higher income to why he is working with such incompetent co-workers, to how he might fail in providing effective leadership on the upcoming project.

At the root of negative self-talk is self-judgment. Self-judgment is characterized by comparing yourself to others, feeling that you are never good enough, or that somehow you require more: more learning, education, support, or more of something.

No one is immune from self-esteem issues. Even the highest of high self-esteem individuals occasionally engage in negative self-talk and self-doubt. Maintaining high self-esteem is an everyday responsibility. Even if a small gesture, I suggest that you do something to enhance your self-esteem each day. Your goal is to continually reinforce to yourself that you are a worthy, valuable person and that the contribution you can make to your organization is worthwhile.

William McGrane, director of the McGrane Self-Esteem Institute in Cincinnati, Ohio, says, "Self-esteem is the greatest influencing factor in our lives." If you don't have an awareness and understanding of the role of self-esteem in your life and in your career, chances are you will not be an effective leader, and you will be thwarted in your ability to influence by design.

What's the Difference, We've Got a Job to Do—"I lead a small group. I'm not sure whether I have a high self-esteem or not. Tomorrow morning, I go to work just like everyone else. Whether my esteem is high or low, and the esteem of my followers is high or low, we have jobs to do and we are going to do them. What's the difference?"

The difference is leading by accident or leading by design! If you are unsure if your esteem is sufficiently high, and would like to raise it here are some tips that will help:

- Identify as honestly as possible your weaknesses. By knowing yourself better and what you are not good at, you may be able to reduce the number of times you compare yourself to others. It is alright for you to be strong in some points and to acknowledge the strengths of others.
- Keep a running log for the next day of each time you catch yourself putting yourself down, in either conversation or thought. As your list of negative statements grows, you will see how this kind of conversation and thinking diminishes your leadership potential.
- Take each phrase that you jotted down and reframe it. For example, if you said to yourself, "I am never going to be able to get my staff to accomplish XYZ" substitute that phrase with, "I am getting stronger and stronger at effectively influencing my staff to accomplish XYZ."
- Practice what Bill McGrane calls "TUA"—total unconditional acceptance of yourself and of other people. As you begin to accept yourself—"this is who I am"—you will find yourself automatically accepting others more readily. If you are 5'8" tall and your dream as a teenager was to reach 6', acknowledge here and now, "I am 5'8" tall, I am never going to be 6' tall." If you have been trying to lose 18 pounds for the last 10 years, I'm not saying stop trying, but acknowledge how much you do weigh and that you feel good about yourself.
- Acknowledge yourself at least once daily for the skills and talents that you bring to the work environment. Acknowledge each of your followers at least once daily for the same.

- Hereafter, throughout the day make affirmations ANY-TIME you catch yourself thinking a negative thought. The subconscious mind doesn't know the difference between what is real and what is imagined, and therefore if you feed it positive thoughts, it will act on those. Even if your affirmation is nothing more complex than, "I am an effective leader," if you say it or think it often enough, your subconscious will continuously work towards that. Here are more affirmations:

  —I work in perfect harmony with my staff.
  —I am an effective leader.
  —I respond well to the needs of my staff.
  —I make a valuable and worthwhile contribution to my organization.
  —I embody tranquility and harmony.
  —I am an understanding, talented, patient leader.
  —I easily maintain my vision and share it with others.
  —My work is more rewarding each day.
  —I am creative and innovative.
  —I am a high-energy person.
  —I feed my body nutritious foods.
  —I readily take action on my ideas.
  —I am an excellent communicator.
  —I have a great sense of humor.
  —I accept others for where and who they are.
  —I live in abundance.
  —I am trusting in myself and in others.
  —I easily identify problems and creatively solve them.
  —I am an emerging expert in my industry.
  —I am more resourceful every day.
  —I feel healthy all the time.
  —I am open to new viewpoints.
  —I attract hardworking dedicated followers.
  —I am well-rewarded for my efforts.
  —I feel comfortable in new or unfamiliar situations.
  —I can easily take vacations!

- If you find yourself rushing throughout the day, slow down. Usually the problem is not best met by working faster or maintaining a constant state of urgency. When you find yourself racing, consider the messages you are giving yourself. Perhaps they include, "I don't have enough time, I don't have enough resources, I don't have the capability." The perception of not having enough, more often than not, is just that, a perception. There are many ways to accomplish a desired end. Rather than beat yourself up for what you may not have, slow down, acknowledge your strengths and available resources, and if necessary, proceed down a different path to accomplish a goal. Consciously taking deep breaths during affirmations also helps center you.

- Actively seek to affirm others. Instead of simply saying to a secretary, "Thanks Marge, you did a great job on this report," affirm Marge by saying, "Marge, I would like to acknowledge you for your professionalism on this report. There were no typos, the margins were neat, it was delivered on time and it really comes across as a high-quality document." By acknowledging Marge's specific efforts you help to raise the esteem of both Marge and yourself. Moreover, you set up a situation where the specific efforts of Marge that you acknowledge are likely to be repeated. Author Michael LeBoeuf, Ph.D., says that the greatest management principle is, "Behavior that is rewarded is repeated." When you acknowledge one of your staff, don't make the age old mistake of following the acknowledgement with a criticism. "I like the job you did, but . . ." Words such as *however, but, nevertheless, though,* tend to act as erasers of whatever came before. Get into the habit of offering affirmations with no erasers attached. For the greatest effect, offer the specific affirmation, stop, and *then walk away.* This enables the other person to own the feeling of being affirmed, with no strings, and it helps build the person's self-esteem as well as yours.

Affirmation by Osmosis—Many organizations mount inspiring, affirming, posters and slogans on the walls. In one organization, when these were first mounted some employees viewed them with skepticism and ridicule. They whispered behind the back of the manager who put them up. At first those slogans were even regarded as corny.

In a number of weeks, though, they simply became part of the overall decor and no one minded them very much. Not so magically, the attitudes and morale of the people in the office improved. Each person's subconscious mind, over several weeks, absorbed the messages that those posters contained, which helped create a more positive, stimulating, encouraging environment.

On a personal basis you can post affirmations and stimulating messages around your office, on your bathroom mirror, in your car, briefcase, calendar, even in your gym locker. Don't worry that after a few days or weeks you don't seem to even notice the message anymore—it is getting through. The principle works the same way as when you post the mission statement.

Affirmation and acknowledgement, as well as reducing negative self-talk are self-esteem enhancing tools. You don't need to be anyone other than yourself. When you try to be or think you can be someone else, you are not being truly yourself. Accept yourself as you are; wonderful things will follow!

LEADERS ARE FREE TO RELEASE THE CHILD WITHIN THEM

Recall when you were five years old and the kind of characteristics that you exhibited. Chances are you were energetic, curious, playful, and highly imaginative. You were probably very spontaneous—you didn't get hung up on rules and protocol and you didn't give yourself negative self-talk. You were action oriented; if you wanted to accomplish something you just started it!

Perhaps you had an imaginary playmate or friend or even if you didn't, you exhibited a type of creativity in your play. You could have a great time with minimal resources. A crayon and a piece of paper, or a marble and a shoe box were all you needed.

As a child, you were probably also very forgiving. You could get into a big squabble with your mother or father, or with a friend, but minutes later forget about the whole thing. You maintained a present moment orientation and didn't hang on to what happened five minutes before, let alone the day or week before. If you were like most children, you were able to see the fun in everyday life. You could laugh without reservation. You could become playful at a moment's notice.

I'm a big advocate of letting our child out more often. In my leadership seminar we play with this idea and help people to see the advantages of being more childlike in the work environment.

Following one of my seminars, a man came up to me afterwards and said, "Your discussion of releasing the child within us was very meaningful for me. I used to believe in Santa Claus as a young child. Earlier in my career, I approached the work day with enthusiasm and lightheartedness. I realize now that I am not having fun on the job anymore. Worse, I find myself not believing in possibilities." Then, with a deep sense of conviction and a sigh of relief he said, "I am going to start having fun again at work. I realize now how important it is for me and my followers."

Much of our childlike behavior can be applied to our careers today. Children are open to new experiences and ready to learn new things. They maintain a sense of wonder about the world and are open to new possibilities. When they approach a new object, they will explore it and toss it around rather than be fearful of it. They don't see the object as a threat to their environment.

What about you and your child within? Are you free on occasion to release it? Do you affirm that child within? Your leadership capability may just depend on it.

LEADERS ARE SKILLED PRESENTERS

As a leader there will be time when you need to make, or will be asked to make, a presentation. The *Book of Lists* states that the number one social fear of most people is standing up and speaking before a group. Number 7 on the list is fear of dying. My experience tells me some *would* rather die than stand up and speak to a group! Effective leaders face this fear and are committed to doing what it takes to make a professional presentation.

The skilled presenter is as prepared as possible, assuming nothing. Remember Murphy's law? It's usually right, isn't it? If you take responsibility for the success of your presentation and plan ahead of time, you will be on your way to assuring its success. Here are guidelines to making your presentations reflect your competency and knowledge:

1. If the presentation is to an outside group, chat with the meeting planner to have a clear understanding of what is expected of you in your comments. Also, find out the composition of the audience (age range, occupations, sex), which previous speakers have addressed the group, how much the audience has paid to attend, if anything, and how large a group is expected.

2. Also ask about room size and layout. Is there a meal or cocktail time planned before the program? Knowing this will help you set the tone of your talk. For example, an after-dinner speech requires more humor to keep the audience involved. If your presentation is within your own organization, you still need as many details as possible.

It has been said that the speaker controls the environ-ment, so don't be shy about requesting the room setup that most facilitates your speaking style. Many people need the security of a lectern to speak, while others are inhibited by it. Know what makes you comfortable and request it.

3. Use a microphone if you are addressing groups with more than 50 people. Men have more resonance in their voices and it may carry sufficiently for even larger groups. However, a microphone will allow both men and women to speak in their natural tone without straining their voices to be heard. It also allows for the use of more voice inflection.

   If audio-visuals are used, request pertinent equip-ment, such as an overhead projector, a flip chart, etc. A "program logistics" form with diagrams of how you prefer the room to be set up will make everyone's life easier if you speak regularly.

4. Even if it's an in-house presentation to your own organi-zation, start your talk on time and end on time. This is especially important if it is in the course of a business day, and lets your followers know that you respect their time.

5. If possible, arrive early and greet some of the group. This gives you an opportunity to ask questions of them and listen to their concerns as well as their expectations of your presentation. Mingle at break time, if there is one.

Once you're ready for the presentation, approach the lectern with energy and vitality. Open with a statement, questions or a story that will capture their attention. Add gestures and positive facial expressions, such as a smile. Use good eye contact and take in as much of the group as possible during your speech.

Follow the old but effective wisdom of telling them what you are going to tell them, tell them, then tell them what you have told them. As you speak, highlight important words and phrases with your voice inflection. Be enthusiastic and excited about your topic! End with an anecdote or an appeal to action that will impact them.

There is nothing wrong with using notes, and many effective presenters swear by them, but do avoid reading your speech. Reading it keeps you from being spontaneous. Don't worry about the butterflies, even professional speakers get them. Don't think of yourself as being nervous. Just think about yourself as being full of creative energy! The longer you stay in a leadership role, the more often you'll probably be giving presentations. Commit now to making this one of your high skill areas.

LEADERS LIVE A BALANCED LIFE

Clients continually ask me what our hottest seminar topics are and it is easy to answer. Remaining high on the list is "The Balancing Act" in which we discuss how to manage the challenges of juggling personal, family, and career life. How is this a leadership issue you ask? You operate as a whole person and if one part of your life is out of balance it affects all other parts. Followers notice.

When your life is out of balance, you feel pressured, tense, drained, even depressed. You lose your leadership edge. Many organizations today recognize that a balanced leader is a more productive, happier leader. Some are already taking responsibility for helping their people deal with these types of issues. With the changes that are facing our society today in both the home and workplace, we will see more and more organizations become responsive to this need area.

Dr. Charles Garfield in his book *Peak Performance* found that even widely acknowledged leaders may not be balanced in all aspects of their lives on a daily basis, but they tend to continually refocus their attention so as to achieve an overall life balance. They are not totally immersed in any one aspect of their lives whether it's work, family or hobbies.

I liken these findings to balancing the tires on your car. If the tread on one tire is low, or if you have a flat, the other three tires won't work well even if they are brand new. In the case of a flat you may not be able to operate the car at all. Use the following chart to help assess and improve upon your personal effectiveness.

PERSONAL EFFECTIVENESS PROFILE*

	Need Improvement			Getting Better		Good			Strong	
	10	20	30	40	50	60	70	80	90	100
Self-awareness										
Enthusiasm										
Energy										
Positive attitude										
Personal poise										
Active listening										
Self-confidence										
Self-motivation										
Creativeness										
Self-discipline										
Flexibility										
Establishment of goals										
Decision-making skills										
Positive action										
Organizational skills										
Management of time										
Calculated risk taking										
Persistence										
Ambition										
Interest in job										
Public speaking ability										
Vocabulary										
Understanding people										
Management of stress										
Personal relationships										
Concern for others										
Balance of life— Personal, family, career										

*Rate yourself from 10 to 100—know your strengths as well as your weaknesses. If you score consistently in the "Needs Improvement" area, ask yourself what steps are necessary to move your score to "Strong" and do something about it!

While some effective leaders have been workaholics, in my experience, generally they are not. A workaholic can be effective as a leader for short-term projects or if he or she is running an entrepreneurial business. Being a workaholic is not desirable for effectively influencing followers or staff by design over the long term, however. It tends to make followers resentful, stressful, or cynical.

THE BALANCED LEADER

It no longer surprises me that more than 90 percent of the characteristics of effective leaders are described by such words as enthusiastic, caring, consistent, honest, a good listener and possessing a good sense of humor. These skills are what we refer to as adaptive skills and basically describe personality characteristics and attitudes.

We all know people who are highly-skilled technically and seem to have a great deal of knowledge in their specific areas, but somehow they can't seem to get along with people very well. A leader with balance will be skilled in the functional areas of the job, and will have industry-specific knowledge. The first thing that others are drawn to, however, is how people project themselves.

When all is said and done, like attracts like; balanced, healthy people attract balanced, healthy people!

PART II

SPREADING THE WORD

In your quest to influence by design there are specific, proactive steps that you can take as well as common barriers to effective communication that you will want to overcome. In Chapter 1, we discussed a variety of challenges confronting today's leader. Yet, excellent companies and strong leaders can still get the best from their people year after year because they operate from a different viewing point. This led to Chapter 2 which explained operating from vision, Chapter 3 on creating a mission statement, and Chapter 4, on maintaining the leadership edge.

In Part II, SPREADING THE WORD, we'll look at how effective leaders visually, vocally and verbally communicate their vision and mission to the followers who can "buy in" and become supportive, productive team members.

At all times, responsibility for the effectiveness of the staff falls back on the shoulders of the leaders. This may be uncomfortable or upsetting to the reader who encounters absenteeism and tardiness, negative attitudes and a plethora of other problems. Organizational or department leadership creates the culture in which employees flourish or merely choose to get by—there is no circumnavigating this reality. So, the next element in successfully leading is to spread the word—convey the essence of the vision and the components of the mission statement throughout the company or department.

What They See Is What You Get   5

Let him who would move the world
first move himself.

Socrates

As a leader, you are on stage every minute during the workday, and often beyond. You are a walking visual, vocal and verbal example to your followers as to how they will act. Everything that you say and do has some influence on your followers. Dr. Janet Elsea, a trainer based in Arizona, says that, "You cannot *not communicate*." Everything you say and do delivers a message. Everything. Your attitude, thoughts and feelings are reflected to your followers through one means or another.

The more you attempt to hide something, the more evident it may become. To effectively articulate the vision, or the precepts of the mission, it is essential to influence by design; to do otherwise is to invite influence by accident, and influencing by accident leads to undesirable outcomes.

THE RISK OF COMMUNICATING

Communicating with consistency is no easy task. In normal human interaction there are many ways to be misinterpreted or to convey a mixed message. You can offer an ambiguous message to your followers without even knowing it. You may make great strides in establishing a vision and a mission but unless you have the ability to communicate and to get others to "buy in," you run the risk of being the only one following the vision and the mission. What point is there in having a plaque on your wall that none of your followers understand? A vision and a mission that your followers don't understand or haven't accepted won't be communicated to your customers.

Communicating a message, particularly one that involves your feelings, is a risky process. No one likes to be rejected. Most people, including leaders, would rather not tell people what they think, believe, or need, rather than risk being rejected. Followers may not like what you have to say, they may not agree with it, they may even privately scorn you.

A leader trying to communicate her vision to followers places herself in a potentially precarious position. This is particularly true if it is a vision that is far beyond what the followers have ever been exposed to or one containing spiritual elements. What if no one responds? What if they see it as mumbo jumbo? It is easier to manage by avoidance or crisis than put yourself out on a limb.

WHEN NEEDS AND WANTS INTERFERE

If you are the type of person who has a need for control or having the last word, you may continually be missing the important aspects of communication. Suppose you have a strong need to look good and you are attempting to convey the mission statement to followers. If it is important for you to have ownership of the mission statement and you are not willing to let others be involved in its development, you incur a lower probability of them buying into it.

The leader who works on the mission statement alone in closed quarters and then dramatically presents it to followers, risks generating a fraction of the enthusiasm he could have otherwise. Do you have a high need to be in charge or to be the star? If so, your ability to influence by design may be severely hampered.

Let's turn to how you can visually, vocally and verbally influence by design.

YOUR VISUAL IMPACT

I cringe when hearing somebody repeat the often-quoted phrase, "You never get a second chance to make the first impression." The reality is *each time* we encounter someone we *make a first impression*. When you walk into the office in the morning you are making a daily first impression. Everything you say and do communicates something. Whatever mood you convey quickly is disseminated throughout your organization or department; it doesn't matter whether you say a word or not.

The mood you convey may not be your fault. You may have a headache. You may have not slept well. You may be facing great personal upheaval. Your body language and facial expressions, however, speak very loudly. Dr. Leonard Zunin, coauthor with Natalie Zunin of *Contact: The First Four Minutes*, has done extensive work in interpersonal communications. He found that a person's positive or negative impressions about another person are formed within the first four minutes. Then, after forming those impressions, a person will spend the rest of the time looking for the reason to validate those first impressions.

According to a study by Dr. Albert Marabian at UCLA, of the four communication modes—seeing, hearing, writing, listening—55 percent of the impact that you will have on someone is based on what they see of you; what you wear, how you look and act, your posture, poise and demeanor, the way you walk, move, sit, and stand, and the gestures you use.

WHAT MESSAGE ARE YOU IMPARTING?

"So I was angry when I walked into the office this morning, big deal. My staff is still employed to do their jobs well." Though we would like to think this, once your people observe your behavior at the start of a day, they tend to emulate it. I call this the lengthening shadow. On a non-conscious level they interpret how you are that morning as *how they are to be.*

If you are angry, they are angry. If you are struggling, they are struggling. Their message is: "It's okay to be like you." The fabulous news is, if you walk into the office every morning with confident strides and an attitude that conveys, "We can handle whatever challenges our organization faces," then that is the message that your followers begin to emulate.

As the leader goes, so go the followers. When you feel good, inspired, and energetic you give people permission to be the same way. *This is how corporate culture is transmitted, and it is never by accident.* If the people at the top convey:

Everything is basically fine,
We believe in our people,
Change is healthy, and
We aim to serve our markets better than anyone,

then that is the culture that begins to develop. Armed with this insight, what would you like to convey to your followers? Here are some suggestions:

- We are doing well now. We are going to do even better.
- Our products and services offer great value.
- We can overcome whatever challenges we face.
- This is a dynamic atmosphere and a great place to work.
- I am happy to be here.
- I wouldn't want to be working any place else.
- I believe in what we are doing.
- We are going to accomplish great things today.
- Everyone here is an important part of the team.

LET'S GET PHYSICAL

The way you move and present yourself physically makes a profound impact on your staff. Your movements make a statement about your energy level, enthusiasm, and passion for your vision. Your stride makes a statement about your level of confidence. You are on stage all the time though you may not want to hear it, and may not choose to accept this role. I have worked with enough leaders, long enough to know that this is how it works. As Roger Ailes says, "You are the message."

Your people continually look to you as a example of how to be. The challenge never stops. If leadership is lonely, it is because few are able to serve as around-the-clock models of behavior. The best leaders, however, are the best models they can be.

MAXIMIZING YOUR VISUAL PRESENCE

Here are fundamental elements to master to have the greatest visual impact when interacting with others:

Directionality—When you stand or sit, face the other person and speak directly to him/her. Not being in alignment with the direction of a staff member or follower takes away from your visual impact. In my seminars, I ask people to literally turn their chairs towards one another and practice being directly in line with another. The fact that you take the time and effort to face someone conveys to that someone that they are important.

Composure—This is a gift we give people when we are communicating with them. It is simply being still. It is not being on the phone, tapping with a pen, fiddling with papers, looking over their shoulder, or making any other kind of movement. Think for a second how you feel when another person is soft and composed with you, so still and so pleasant with you that nothing else is moving. They are reading your non-visual but ever-present sign which says:

MAKE ME FEEL IMPORTANT

Facial Affect—The most important thing that can be said about facial expressions is—please have some! Particularly when your eyes have no expression, *you* have no expression. I don't know if the eyes are the window to the soul, but they are the window to good interpersonal communication.

If you are not connecting with your eyes, you are not connecting. To be present with someone is to spend the majority of the time with them looking at them, not in a fixated, staring manner but in an active, engaging manner.

A Smile—It is difficult when someone is smiling at us to not give a smile back. Some leaders would rather do anything than smile, yet it costs nothing, requires very few muscles, and wins followers by the legions. A smile conveys a sense of aliveness and approval.

Posture—Whether sitting or standing your posture conveys an attitude. When standing, if you are leaning on one foot, or if one hip is bearing more weight than the other, you are defusing your power. People tend to pay more attention and listen more closely to speakers who have an erect symmetrical stand. Whether standing or sitting, balance your weight evenly. Keep your shoulders back, and face forward.

Despite leaning back in his chair in every conceivable direction, William F. Buckley, Jr. is a highly influential person on his show, "Firing Line." Imagine his impact, however, if he sat up squarely to lambast his opponent's point of view.

Use of Personal Space—Our personal energy radiates about five feet out from us in all directions and is not based on our size. As speaker and trainer Patricia Ball says, "You can be 6'4" and 240 pounds and emanate weakness, or 5'2" and petite and emanate power." Some people just seem to take up space. The first time I saw the slight, petite Mother Theresa, I was amazed by her powerful presence. When she entered the room she seemed to take up all the space. Her energy filled the room and everyone noticed it.

Conversely, we all encounter people who have been in a room with others, for hours, and nobody notices them. As a leader, you want to expand your energy space—it doesn't take away from others, it helps them to see you more easily.

There are different types of personal space. Intimate space is about 18 inches. Getting into somebody's intimate space before you are invited can be very confronting. If you are tall or large you need to be even more careful. Some people will feel confronted even if you're beyond 18 inches from them, whereas a smaller person may be closer than 18 inches with no problem.

When interviewing someone you want to have as few barriers as possible. If your goal is to connect with this person and have a stronger measure of interpersonal communication, you want to strip away psychic or physical barriers—this includes desks, tables, counters and so forth. People who don't really want others near them use desks and tables and other barriers, on an unconscious level, to keep others at a distance.

Executives who bury themselves behind large desks and conduct all transactions across it, are using them as fortresses. Often, I ask if I can take a chair from across the desk and move it to the side of the desk so at least we are conversing over the front left- or front right-hand corner.

If you want to maintain a comfortable posture but don't want to appear too open or direct, then sit or stand at right angles to one another. This is less confronting, maintains some semblance of directionality, and is entirely acceptable in business. If you are giving a performance appraisal never sit side-by-side with the person. This positions you as a peer or an equal which makes for an ineffective review.

The Handshake—The handshake says to another person, "Welcome to my world," or "I am only doing this because I have to." Presented well, it can convey an array of positive messages including:

- I am glad to see you.
- It is nice to meet you.
- I am looking forward to this meeting.
- I am confident in what I have to say.
- I feel good about myself.

Many people don't know how to shake hands properly. Some men today are still uncomfortable extending a hand to a woman. They are really not sure what to do. Few hard and fast rules exist other than to be courteous.

When shaking hands with a staff member or follower, particularly someone you have greeted often, a host of variations are permissible. The handshake can be firm, short and sweet. You can bounce. You can cover the person's hand with your other hand. In any case, your attitude is always showing, and the message always gets through.

YOUR VOCAL IMPACT

How you speak to others has much more impact than what you actually say. Dr. Albert Marabian found that your tone of voice accounts for 38 percent of the impact of your message to another person. Tone of voice includes:

- volume—how loud or soft you are;
- rate of speech—how fast or slow, and
- pitch—how high or low.

What does your vocal impact have to do with your ability to spread the word? It has everything to do with it. Your followers may not always get your message through the words you offer, but they always get the message by your tone of voice. Add body language to tone of voice and you offer an unmistakable message, regardless of what you are actually saying.

Your tone of voice sets the tone for the conversation. Others will get defensive, tense, defused, or supportive based on the way you speak to them. If you think this is obvious, consider that whenever you speak about vision, if your enthusiasm, commitment, and energy isn't evident, you may well be offering a mixed message to others.

AVOIDING THE POWER ROBBERS

Here are two basic ways some leaders defuse their power:

Insufficient Volume—If you speak too softly when the situation calls for volume your ability to influence may decrease.

Speaking Too Quickly—While a strong emotional appeal laced with enthusiasm is recommended, if your words are offered too quickly or if you lack pause power, the impact of your message can be defused. If you are the type of person who speaks quickly when you get excited, you have to walk the fine line between speaking at too great a pace for people to follow, and too slowly, which may reduce your overall effectiveness. Passive communication begets passivity, while energy begets energy.

TONES THAT LEAD

One of your greatest challenges as a leader is to speak with high energy tones. If your followers hear or see little else other than your energy, you may still be an effective leader because you tend to receive that which you are transmitting. As a speaker, I'm hired for my high energy as well as my particular message. The energy that you convey and transmit as a leader, particularly through your tone of voice, leaves an indelible impression on those taking their cues from you. Energy begets energy!

I don't know who is teaching that stuff about leaders never showing emotion. The most dynamic, inspirational leaders that I've known have been able to rally the troops with a tone of voice and a body language that says, "This excites me; I hope it excites you. I think we have great opportunity here."

"So do I have to be a cheerleader?" In some respects, yes. Many leaders don't want to show great emotion. They think it is beneath them, or that somehow it will convey the wrong image. Some have been taught that showing or displaying emotion is not acceptable, that it is more appropriate to show a cool, stoic, even calculated posture. You can play it that way, but you're in danger of never achieving your full potential as a leader.

To inspire others to go to the beyond requires an appeal to their emotions. One of the great lessons that Jimmy Carter learned during his presidency is that people seldom respond purely to facts, logic, and rational thinking. The basic appeal that you can offer will come through your tone of voice. Yes, there have been effective leaders throughout history, such as Dwight Eisenhower, who did not outwardly display high enthusiasm, but the odds favor those who do.

Ralph Waldo Emerson said, "Nothing great has been achieved without enthusiasm." How great a leader do you want to be? The answer depends on how much enthusiasm you're willing to show.

VERBAL COMMUNICATION

Verbal communication encompasses the words that we choose, and our ability to articulate which involves using the tongue, lips, teeth and throat. Dr. Marabian found that this component of interpersonal communication accounts for only 7 percent of the impact that one person has on an another.

LEVELS OF VERBAL COMMUNICATION

We communicate with others at one of six levels and the more deeply we proceed into these levels, the more effective our communication is with another person and the more we build rapport and form a common union.

1. **Small talk**—This is simply saying, "Hello," or, "How are you doing?" to people in the hallways. Not much is involved with small talk, but it's better than silence or ignoring people.
2. **Talking about people and things**—This is conversation with a focus away from either of the two parties in the conversation. The focus could be on world events, the latest sports scores, somebody else in the organization, or anything else directed away from yourself. This is a safe level of conversation from the standpoint of revealing the inner you—you are not revealing anything about yourself.
3. **Sharing opinions, thoughts and ideas**—At this level you are willing to expose a little bit more of yourself. You reveal some inner-held thoughts. It is a little risky—there is always a chance that the other party may reject your ideas, or criticize you. Usually, at the first indication that the other party may not agree with us, we tend to go back to the earlier, safer second level of conversation.

4. **Emotional conversation**—When you have been hurt or threatened, or become angry, your emotions take over. The conversation and tone of voice are of a much different nature than any of the previous three levels. Jealousy, as well as positive emotions such as excitement, can trigger this level of conversation.

5. **Conversation about feelings**—At this level you discuss what you are feeling, and who you are. Note, there is a difference between your emotions talking, and talking about your emotions. At this level you are able to express your doubts or fears, sorrows or your joys. You might express what you need or what you want. This type of conversation helps nurture personal, emotional growth because you begin to learn more about yourself as you express yourself. You also help others to know you better, because you are indicating what you need and what you feel, information which people are not always willing to share.

   This level of conversation generally only takes place between people who have an evolving relationship. This type of conversation comes as a result of your building deeper rapport with others, and helps to build deeper rapport in itself.

6. **Intimacy**—This is also known as peak communication. These are the very rare moments when you are perfectly in tune with another person. You have a sense of emotional fulfillment because you know that the other person really does get what you are saying. Larry Wilson, the noted trainer and author, breaks down the word "intimacy" into four words: "in to me see."

   Intimacy is allowing another to see the unmasked, unprotected, imperfect you. The reason why we don't generally converse at the peak communication level is because we don't want people to see into us. With 96% of Americans coming from dysfunctional families, more people tend to be hiding who they are. Hence intimate conversation has a diminished chance of occurring.

When you get to this level of conversation with another person, particularly as a leader speaking to followers, it is a very rare and often wonderful moment. To become a master at influencing by design you need to be able to get to people in a way that allows them to see you as leader and as a person on a deep level. Some leaders, and many people in general, never engage in the sixth level of conversation (intimacy) in their entire lives. Some people are able to get to this level with a spouse or significant other but with no one else.

On rare occasion, you may experience someone coming right up to you and conversing at the sixth level, just like that. Following some presentations, when I really connected with the audience, people have come up to me who felt like I was talking directly to them and begun conversing at the sixth level. It happens more often with women than men, but I do get a fair number of men who come up. Men have more trouble expressing themselves on a deep emotional level; some studies reveal that it is actually easier for women to communicate in today's world than it is for men.

CONVERSING AT A HIGH LEVEL

To create an effective relationship with those you seek to lead, and to effectively spread the word, requires making the time to get to know people and building a relationship such that you can converse with them at a high level. You may not get to level six, but you may develop a better capability for expressing thoughts, ideas, and opinions with each other.

The ability to tell another person what you believe, what you think, what you need and what you want is a masterstroke of interpersonal communication and high self-esteem. When two people can offer such expression to one another and not be threatened, they have the basis for a very high-level interaction.

Forming A Common Union Through Active Listening

6

People won't care how much you know until they know how much you care.

Cavett Robert

Listening is the most important, least understood, and most troublesome of all the communication skills. Fortunately, most listening problems can be overcome by having the right attitudes, according to author Dr. Robert Conklin. "There is no such thing as uninteresting people," says Conklin, "only uninterested listeners," or, people with inflexible listening habits. You can become a better listener and make it pay off as a leader too.

Starting with the benefits of effective listening, let's explore the art of listening, with emphasis on helping you to become a better listener and then helping your followers to become better listeners.

BENEFITS OF LISTENING EFFECTIVELY

There are at least six major benefits to listening effectively, including:

Improved management skills when dealing with employees who have problems—You may not be able to solve the problems, but whatever communication you have with them will be improved through effective listening.

Decreased time spent in solving problems—Getting directions or information correctly yields great benefits all the way down the line.

Increased self-esteem and self-confidence because you relate more effectively with others—When you actively and earnestly listen to another person, automatically your self-esteem and self-confidence rise because you are giving a gift to another and quite simply, it feels good to give. Concurrently, their opinion of you rises because you take the time to listen.

Increased productivity, more information rendered, and decreased misunderstanding—One of the most costly aspects of business is poor listening, which contributes to errors, down time, misdirection, and hampered productivity. Active listening improves the chances of doing the job right the first time.

Fewer mistakes made because you listened to the instructions—Whether it is taking an appliance out of a box for the first time, or getting instructions from another person, we all have a tendency to run before we can walk. The fastest road to fewer mistakes, however, is following instructions.

Increased respect, trust, and rapport with coworkers—To listen to others intently is to honor them. They in turn will honor you. You can't help but have better relations with followers who know you are listening to them.

BARRIERS TO EFFECTIVE COMMUNICATION

To enjoy the benefits often requires overcoming some obstacles. Of the endless number of barriers to effective listening and interpersonal communication, here are some common ones which you may identify with:

Speaking too much, listening too little—All people have an inborn tendency to want to hear themselves. The danger, when communicating your vision and mission to your followers, is that if you do not listen to them, you won't know the degree to which they understand and accept what you've said. The only way you can be totally present to your followers is to give them your full and undivided attention, an act which takes considerable practice. If you are too concerned with getting your own words out, you won't be concerned enough with what your followers are saying to you.

Personal values interfere with true meaning—Any personal pressures, prejudices, or social or economic barriers on the part of you or your listener may cause static in the communication process. In a society of increasing multi-ethnic diversity, this factor is critical and will grow in importance. What seems to you to be a simple statement with a clear message, may not be simple and clear to others.

More than ever, effective leadership necessitates ensuring that your followers understand everything. Take nothing for granted when it comes to effectively communicating your message. When you need to let people know what is expected of them, where the company or division is going, or what you want to have happen in this department, recognize that followers may misunderstand your message because of the way they interpret one single word:

Ask a group of ten people what they hear when they hear the word, "fire." Three or four may think of hot flames. Some may think of termination from a company.

Another may think of someone shooting a gun, while another may think of becoming motivated or fired up.

Misinterpreting nonverbal cues—Your nonverbal responses can be just as important as verbal responses, and on some level we all understand this. The last time you explained to someone how to do something, did he or she say, "Yes, I understand. I'll take care of it," only to return with the job partially or completely wrong? Were there identifiable cues in his behavior that revealed his real level of understanding, such as a quizzical facial expression?

Sometimes because of your authority, others will decline to tell you that they do not understand what you have just said. Some followers don't listen well and others are just in a hurry to get on to the next item. Do you have the patience to ask your staff members to repeat the instructions, and to listen to what they say? If not, you may be spending considerably more time later when your directions have not been followed.

Being closed to new ideas—We all evaluate new ideas and suggestions from our own point of view, which can be limiting. Someone describes a new way to do something and it doesn't fit within the context of our understanding, so we summarily reject it, when the new way could be a better way. Often, we reach preconceived conclusions based on our prior experience and mentally exit before the other person has finished explaining his approach. This is a tragedy of everyday communications. The people reporting to us have specific, first-hand knowledge of the subject matter—they are the ones on the front line.

The longer you have been in your present position, and the more established you are within the organization, the greater the tendency may be for you to take mental exits from conversations. To lead effectively in a climate of change let your employees lead you on occasion. Unless you create the environment in which others will share gems with you, you'll never be exposed to them.

Interrupting subordinates—This occurs frequently but not necessarily because of rudeness. Often, we have to dash off to the next meeting or believe we know the conclusion to someone's message. Since the typical person speaks at a rate of 125 to 175 words per minute and we think at a rate of 500 to 700 words per minute it's easy to get bored or frustrated. If you don't have the time or capability to listen to someone all the way through, then *don't engage in conversation until you can.*

Taking mental vacations—Because of the ability to listen and think at a much faster rate than people normally speak we sometimes entertain a variety of thoughts while someone else is speaking. This serves very little purpose—we don't hear what another is actually saying, and we don't have well-formed conclusions about what else we were thinking.

Sometimes an employee makes a statement which triggers something else within us. Then, bingo, we go on a mental vacation which might last a few seconds, one minute, or longer. However long, we literally do not hear the person during that time. Sure enough, she mentions something crucial and the next day she checks back with us about it, but we have no idea why. This is a continuing cause of friction. The follower knows she mentioned it; the leader insists that she didn't.

DIFFERENT TYPES OF LISTENERS

Often, barriers to listening occur because of a person's predisposed style of listening. There are at least four different types of listeners, including the non-focused listener, the marginal listener, the evaluative listener, and finally, the active listener—the only one who actually gets full messages.

The non-focused listener—The non-focused listener isn't really listening to you. He is staring at the wall or contemplating what he wants to say. This type of listener is prone to interrupt and often has the need to get in the last word. To placate you, he may offer fake attention. However, often he offers no signs that he's making an effort to listen to you.

The non-focused listener is more interested in *who you know* than *what you know*. Understandably he tends to be disliked, if tolerated, by others.

The marginal listener—This person hears the sounds you make, but the not the real message. He stays on the surface without risking real communication with you. He may listen for facts while not grasping ideals. Like the non-focused listener, the marginal listener may offer clues that he doesn't regard what you are saying as important. He is easily distracted and ready to give other things attention. Because the marginal listener often postpones dealing with problems he ends up making things more difficult than if he simply listened effectively in the first place and dealt with the issues being presented.

The evaluative listener—This listener remains emotionally detached from you. She hears you but she doesn't catch your intention. She is more concerned with the context of your message. She often ignores body language, tone of voice and facial expressions which could add to her understanding. Evaluative listeners are often good at ingesting factual and statistical information but lack the sensitivity to perceive the full impact of your message.

The non-focused listener, marginal listener, and **evaluative listener** may all contribute to errors in communications, lost sales, employee dissatisfaction, and lower productivity. As one moves from non-focused listening to active listening, the potential for trust, understanding and effective communications increases.

The active listener—This listener is interested in effective communication and is willing to work at understanding the other person's point of view. This person is attentive to both words and feelings, and both verbally and non-verbally reveals that he/she is listening. He uses his eyes, head, expressions and gestures as well as personal space to convey that what you have to say is important.

The active listener doesn't tend to interrupt—he lets the other person have the floor. All the while, he is seeking to gain a deep understanding of the other person, employing all of his perceptive skills. Many active listeners also are skillful questioners. They respond to what another has to say by offering perceptive questions and other feedback. They let the other person fully express himself.

The active listener is comfortable with silence. He doesn't feel the need to jump in if the other party pauses for a moment. His goal is to get a deeper understanding of the person speaking and of the message being conveyed. People like to be around active listeners because everyone likes to think that what they have to say is important.

ACTIVE LISTENING STRATEGIES

It's difficult to influence people if you're not willing to actively listen to them. Here are some strategies for conveying to your followers that you are an active listener:

Open the Door—When you open the door to communication others perceive you as an active listener. Offer your followers an invitation to talk by asking, "Care to tell me about it?," or "Your face is beaming today," which naturally will elicit a response and get the other person to open up.

After indicating your willingness to listen, also indicate that you're willing to wait a bit by offering silence. Give the other person time to decide whether to talk and, if so, what he wants to say. Use eye contact and posture which shows that you have both time and attention when the other person would like to speak to you.

Encourage the Speaking—Once the other person has started talking, offer rejoinder words and phrases that both help and encourage him to continue, such as:

Tell me more.	Oh?	Yes!
For instance . . .	Really?	I see . . .
You bet!	Gosh!	Go on . . .
And then what?	Right!	Then?
You're kidding!	Wow!	Mmmm . . .

Ask Questions—Ask either open-ended or closed-ended questions. An example of a closed-ended question is, "Do you want to see me about the Smith file?" or, "Did you enjoy the luncheon?" These are questions which may invite more discussion but initially only ask for specific response.

As often as possible, attempt to ask open-ended questions which indicate to followers that you are interested in their views and observations, and *regard them as more than just reporting mechanisms.* Open-ended questions such as, "What's on your mind, Bill?" or, "How did the meeting go?" invite discussion and give the other person the lead in the conversation.

Paraphrase—When you paraphrase another person you offer a concise response which states her message in your own words. Paraphrasing conveys active listening because it gives the other person an immediate summary of your understanding of what she said. If you haven't listened, you can't paraphrase effectively.

Generally, any communication can be paraphrased. Here is the paraphrase of the sentence preceding this one: "Usually, whatever someone says can be said a different way." Some people shun paraphrasing because they feel as if it makes them sound foolish. Yet, it's one of the most effective ways I know to make an indelible impression on another.

Reflect the Speaker's Feelings—Related to paraphrasing is mirroring back to the speaker the emotions which are being communicated. Suppose someone says to you, "Darn it! Why can't I get phone calls on time?" To reflect the speaker's feelings you could say to him, "It sounds like you're upset because someone didn't return a call."

Summarize—A final technique for conveying your active listening is to briefly re-state the main themes and feelings that the speaker expressed over a lengthy conversation. Suppose Joe finishes talking to you after several minutes. You would then offer the statement, "It is my understanding, then, that XYZ. Is that correct?" The summary can be a paraphrase, a reflection of the speaker's feelings or meaning, or combination of paraphrase and reflection. You make it clear through your summary that you've been following the other person all along.

USING QUESTIONS TO CONVEY YOUR INTEREST

Not all questions are created equal. Depending on your relationship with the other person, and the degree of interaction you choose, the questions you ask will vary in nature and intensity. The five levels of questions include safe questions, closed questions, open questions, interview questions, and congruent questions.

Safe Questions—Many leaders employ simple questions that help draw out information and help the other person relax. They are easy to answer, and because of their relative effortlessness, make the other person feel comfortable with you. Responses don't require deep thought, technical analysis, or calculations.

Safe questions frequently appear in the form of greetings, small talk, and incidental conversation. Their primary role is to release tension and allow a deeper level of communication to ensue.

Closed Questions—Closed questions, referred to earlier, are requests for one- or two-word responses. A true and false, yes and no, or multiple choice question is a closed question. These are valuable for obtaining specific facts and information.

Closed questions often begin with the words *what, are, do, who, where,* or *which, i.e.,* where did you go?, do you like blue or green?, are you coming tomorrow? Used exclusively, closed questions may make people feel as if they are being interrogated. They are best used in combination with other types of questions.

Open Questions—Open questions allow the other person to elaborate. I like to think of them as short essay questions. They cause the other person to share because of your interest. Open questions can be used to increase another's personal energy or to uncover a hot button—what is of interest to him/her. Open questions start with *what, how,* and *in what way.*

For example:

"How is that new regulation going to affect us?"
"What are your views on Henderson's report?"
"In what way do we come out on top?"

Interview Questions—These are used to focus on a particular area and to gain more depth, often in an interview situation. Interview questions allow you to get closer to another person, and help to surface values and opinions. Interview questions may represent a combination of both open and closed questions. They are more intellectual than feeling. For example, "Why did you decide to leave the Hager Company after eight years?" or, "How do you see yourself contributing to the production team?"

Congruent Questions—Congruent questions are rare. These are questions that go to the core of what the other party is telling you. They may not always be comfortable for you to ask, or for the other party to answer. With trust, support and a high skill level, the other person may be more encouraged to respond.

If you have ever experienced such a question, you can clearly recall the words spoken, the time of day, place, person and outcome of the interaction. Certainly these are not an everyday event. They involve feelings and often provoke great passion on the part of the person being asked the question. In our society, men have difficulty with this level of questioning, because it deals with feelings; all too often they have not been taught to deal with feelings.

LISTENING MAKES A DIFFERENCE

Check yourself on the following questions to see if you use active listening to get the most out of your relationships:

1.	Do you know at least a little something about the interests of each person whom you lead?	Yes	No
2.	Do you tend to be patient when listening to your followers?	Yes	No
3.	Are you generally a cheerful and enthusiastic listener?	Yes	No
4.	Do you convey both verbal and non-verbal cues when listening?	Yes	No
5.	Can you refuse another's request without making him/her feel antagonistic towards you?	Yes	No
6.	Do you offer followers the reasons behind your directives?	Yes	No
7.	Do you ask your followers for their opinions?	Yes	No
8.	Do you mix both open and closed questions in your communication?	Yes	No
9.	Are you slow to interrupt?	Yes	No
10.	Do you actively encourage others to speak?	Yes	No

11.	Do you paraphrase, reflect, and summarize?	Yes	No
12.	Do your followers consider you to be an effective listener?	Yes	No

PRACTICE LISTENING? YES!

Like any skill, active listening takes practice. Here is an exercise you can practice at home or the office to improve your active listening skills. With a partner, choose one of the suggested openings listed below and give your opinions, ideals, feelings, etc. Your partner is to listen with empathy. After two minutes, switch roles and repeat the process.

Suggested openings:

- I believe in . . .
- The emotion I find most difficult to control is . . .
- My biggest challenge at work is . . .
- I am afraid of . . .
- The thing that concerns me most about change is . . .
- When I disagree with someone, I . . .
- When I am in a new group, I
- The thing that turns me off the most is . . .
- The characteristic that I would like to change about myself is . . .
- I am happiest when . . .

After both of you have had a turn, have the original listener paraphrase, reflect, or summarize what the other person said.

Were either or both of you able to convey the essence of what you were told? To further strengthen your active listening, choose another one of the ten phrases and repeat the process.

HELPING OTHERS TO BE
BETTER LISTENERS

Occasionally, when I speak to groups, unannounced I will pull out a brief article from *Time* or *Newsweek* and say, "This was in *Time* magazine last week. You may or may not have seen it. I would like to share it with you . . ." Then I will read the article, pause, and say, "I'd like to ask you ten questions about the article. Will each of you take out a piece of paper?" I ask them where the story took place and who was involved— straightforward questions.

Following this brief quiz, we review the answers. I ask the audience who got five or more right. Invariably, no one does. Then we begin talking about what just transpired. Without fail, someone says, "We didn't know you were going to ask us about the story." Or, "You didn't announce when you first started that there was going to be a quiz following the story." We go through a long list of reasons they didn't hear the story:

- "We didn't think that there was going to be anything in it for us."
- "You didn't announce what you were doing."
- "We didn't identify with anyone in the story."

Next, I take another article from *Time* or *Newsweek* and tell them, "I'm going to read you another story and I'm going to ask you some questions afterwards." I also mention that they may take notes. Then I read the article and offer the quiz. As you can guess, everyone does remarkably well compared to the first quiz. The difference is they know what the rules are. They know what is expected of them, they know what they can do to prepare themselves, and they know how they will be scored.

WHAT'S IN IT FOR ME?

In a like manner, when working with one of your employees or followers, when you say, "I'm going to present some information to you and this will be essential for you to accomplish XYZ," you raise the probability that he will listen closely and use the information more effectively.

If one of your followers tells you something and initially you don't recognize what's in it for you, you'll miss half of what she is saying. Later, when she refers to the information again (her form of quizzing you) you won't score very well.

If the above information tells us anything, it is that to help your followers become better listeners, always give them the *what's in it for me* (them) information they need in advance of what you are going to tell them. People have a need to know why they are being told something and how it fits. More than that, they need to be able to see *what's in it for them*—no one ever does anything unless they can see what's in it for them. The leadership task is to reward followers by giving them information and telling them in advance how it is going to benefit them—what's in it for them.

PART III:

LEADING THROUGH EMPOWERMENT

The word empowerment has been known to startle many a leader. I can hear many of you now, "Give up control? Let my staff take over and make decisions? No way." Hold on a minute. Empowerment is nothing more than giving people *their* power, not yours.

When you empower another what are you really doing? You are *giving them a chance to tap into their own power*. It is allowing them to do their best work, to function in an environment where they have the freedom to use their talents. As with so much of effective leadership, your high self-esteem is the key to your ability to successfully empower others. You need to be comfortable with yourself and with the strength of others for empowerment to work. Empowerment is not compliance—there is a big difference between your staff doing something to fulfill your expectations, and wanting to do it.

STEPS TO EMPOWERMENT

The basic principle of empowerment, according to Ron Zemke, is that "The person doing the job knows far better than anyone else the best way to do the job," and thus is also the best person to improve it. Leaders need to establish boundaries for followers, and "then get out of the way."

To establish an environment where empowerment can occur, here are seven elements:

Hire the Best People for your organization or department—the best, in this case, meaning consistent with your values and mission. Take time when interviewing. Employ solid interviewing skills to hire the people who are in alignment with the values and culture of your organization and department. Don't just hire a "warm body." (We will explore finding and keeping winners in Chapter 9.)

Communicate Your Expectations—This starts during the initial job interview and is an ongoing process. Be open, accessible and ready to help. Maintain a free flow of information; be ready to handle all questions. Listen, ask questions, and give feedback. Use self-disclosure, empathetic listening, and observation.

Provide Training and Development—Go beyond technical knowledge. Teach people how to like themselves and others. Continue to provide information, resources, and support as your followers need them. Foster an environment of harmony, fun, and productivity. Make life-long learning a commitment in your organization or department. Help your followers to develop their attitudes, knowledge, and skills.

Delegate—To delegate means to entrust the task or authority to someone else. While much has been written on this, delegation continues to be a sore spot with many otherwise effective leaders. We suggest you assign more than simply the tasks you dislike doing. Focus on what will also increase the skills and experience of your followers. Delegation requires high self-esteem and trust. It also means allowing others to make their own mistakes and be accountable for them. Which leads us to . . .

Hold Your Staff Accountable—Let your staff be free to succeed and to make mistakes. Enable them to have ownership over what they do. Set deadlines and establish consequences if work isn't completed. Your followers need to accept the consequences of their behavior and performance, both positive and negative (see Chapter 10, "Developing Self-Directed Followers").

Follow Up through Coaching—The job of the coach is never finished. Even your star performers need coaching. Remember that Olympic athletes travel with their coaches to all major competitions. Coaching occurs (covered in Chapter 11) on an as-it-happens basis, and is best not deferred to some later time when its impact is greatly reduced. Identify the issue and make suggestions for improvements. Let people know what needs to be done differently and specify how to do it. Ask many questions, and carefully listen to and process your followers' responses.

Acknowledge and Reward Your Team—People will channel their energy toward what they are rewarded for or paid to do. The reward you offer can be simple, even in the form of recognition and affirmations. Financial compensation or complex reward systems are not usually necessary. A specific and simple thank you, with eye contact, can work wonders. Nice notes and thoughtful gifts, in addition to fair compensation, tell others that you appreciate their contributions. Everyone wants and appreciates recognition for the good work that they do.

In Chapter 7 we'll discuss the basic building block of empowerment—trust. Specifically we'll look at how to build a leader-follower relationship based on the four key components of trust—openness, acceptance, congruence, integrity. In Chapter 8, we'll discuss how empowering others gives them the opportunity to come into the full presence of their own creative power. With empowerment, you help others to determine what is important for them and how to clarify and identify the work they do best—their "best work."

In Chapter 9, "Finding and Keeping Winners," we'll look at how to staff your department with employees or followers who can latch on to your vision and support your mission. Regardless of their skill levels, many of the people whom you interview will not represent a good fit on your team, not because they lack the fundamental experience, education or training, but because they are not or apparently will not be in alignment with what your organization or team is trying to accomplish.

Chapter 10 presents a new and exciting concept: Developing empowered, self-directed followers, the culmination of your role as leader.

EMPOWERMENT QUIZ

1.   Do you know the "best work" of each of your staff?
2.   What have you done in the past week to empower them?
3.   Are you committed to life-long learning in your organization?
4.   Have you told that employee what you would like done differently, or have you just told someone else about it?
5.   What can you do today to acknowledge and reward your staff?
6.   What would it take for **you** to feel empowered in your work?

Building Trust 7

*If you would lift me, you must be
on higher ground.*
Ralph Waldo Emerson

T o improve your ability to lead your followers, increase
the level of trust between you and them. There are four components to building trust—openness, acceptance, congruence,
integrity. In this chapter we'll examine each component in
detail.

OPENNESS

Openness is a willingness to try new things, listen to new
ideas, and tolerate ambiguity and change. It means maintaining non-judgmental attitudes and behavior, and clearing out
preconceived notions and routine responses to a changing
world. Openness means giving your followers appropriate
information, previously discussed at length. More than that, it
is not hiding anything—people always find out about what
you are withholding from them.

It is infinitely more desirable to have information that impacts your followers come from you than from the grapevine.
Impart information as it becomes available, when it is safe for

the security and competitive position of the organization to have it released, and as all the pieces come together. Otherwise, you run the risk of having to retract what you have put out, or worse, causing followers to act on misinformation.

What if the news you have to offer is completely negative? It still makes more sense to share it with your team than to have them operate in an environment of suspicion and perhaps find out the news from other sources. Remember, you cannot *not* communicate. Maintaining an air of openness is an act of high self-esteem for a leader.

OPENNESS WITH COMPASSION

A company was closing its doors forever after 23 years in operation. One of the managers, who had been with the company for about 18 years, was devastated when he first heard the news from his supervisor. The company, however, always maintained openness with its employees. They created a six-month decompression phase offering individual counseling for employees, helping them with job searches, offering a fair severance compensation program and making the final days as painless as possible. That's compassion.

A wise leader *knows each of his followers; he knows when and how to deliver information to each of them.* Some people are able to receive new information as it happens; they understand the big picture and are able to integrate new data. Others on your staff may have to be handled more gently. They don't understand the big picture and while you don't intend to withhold information from them, it's best for all concerned to dispense it to them in a manner that is comfortable for them. The only way you can do this is to understand the individual needs and characteristics of those whom you lead.

What if you don't have the whole story? To build trust, you need to be as open and as forthright as possible. Tell them the pieces that you have and tell them what you are working on.

If you convey only partial truth, you run the risk of having them get other answers from other sources. You never want to be in a situation where your followers suspect that you are leaving something out intentionally, because this opens up the door to greater suspicion next time.

YOUR BODY TALKS

In addition to what you are telling them, people are always reading your body language. As we saw in Chapter 5 you are always giving visual and vocal cues. What you say is not nearly as convincing as how you deliver it.

Have you ever watched a television news bulletin where a spokesperson from the U.S. State Department addresses an audience of reporters and broadcasters? The audience *knows* what parts of the report are factual or not—they can feel it. When vital information is being left out, reporters go into a frenzy, vehemently trying to get all the details, and the full story. No matter how well the spokesperson is trained to calmly deliver the essence of a situation, the audience knows when there is more to this story than first meets the ear.

In a company in the southwest, which shall also remain nameless, the president took a physical examination and was diagnosed as having a terminal disease. The executive staff panicked and decided that employees of the large organization would not be able to handle such news. Following his well-publicized operation, which came after months of declining health, the company's public relations department issued a news release saying that the operation was a success, the surgeons were able to eradicate the problem, and that the president would be back on his feet in no time.

I watched the TV broadcast when the company spokesperson delivered this news at a press conference. As good as he was at presenting the information, his body language said that this is not the real story, and he was afraid to tell you the complete story. We can all understand why top management wanted to maintain an image of continuity and stability. Yet everyone knew that his message lacked the ring of truth.

Having disseminated false information, and attempting to uphold it, the company was beset with more problems. In the following weeks and months rumors began to fly. Rather than maintain a posture of stability, the facade resulted in a major backfire. Long-term employees were visibly shaken. Conflicting reports from the grapevine buffeted their confidence and trust in the executive staff. As more time passed, the company president began "communicating" only through memos and printed materials. Reporters picked away at the truth and the entire community became concerned. The price of the company's stock declined.

The irony is that the executive staff thought that they would face a terrible fate by revealing the truth, whereas they probably experienced a more terrible fate by not disclosing the truth. Would you rather influence by accident or by design? During what is obviously a harrowing period, would you rather have the opportunity to engender the support of the employees, or keep them in a constant state of suspicion where very little support from them, if any, can be offered?

You can't run away from the truth. In the long run it's the only thing that really works. You can determine how to express it in a compassionate way, but you can't step around it.

In another case, a company was sold and was in the process of being transferred to the new owners. This represented a positive, healthy change for the organization. The company would be afforded more resources and gain a more competitive position in the marketplace. Still, top management recognized that the changes necessitated a transition period. While no jobs were lost and indeed many positions were upgraded, leaders from the old and new parent organization maintained an atmosphere of openness and continually demonstrated a willingness to assist team members with this important shift in operations. Leaders build trust at all opportunities.

PRACTICE SELF-DISCLOSURE

By revealing your concerns and offering some self-disclosure you further engender trust among your followers. Many leaders, who can impart the truth, but can't be open about their own feelings, are only marginally effective at influencing by design.

As a party to the process of change, you will have feelings and emotions about the change just as your followers do. Inject a part of yourself so that others can follow more easily. Here are some catch phrases that you can use:

- I am really excited about this . . .
- When I first learned of this I realized we were going to be facing some tough challenges . . .
- I was shaken when I learned _____ but now I understand that the opportunity before us is achievable.
- I wouldn't want to face this with anyone else but you.
- You know, I have been pretty comfortable myself in the way that we have been doing _____. Now it is time to move on.
- Like you, I am concerned that the parent organization may not understand . . .
- At first I had deep reservations about this, but _____
- When I got the new instructions, I was very confused at first. After a little while though _____

Offer small parenthetical asides that let workers know that you too had personal challenges to overcome before you accepted whatever change is being discussed.

Remember the scene in "The Ten Commandments" where the Egyptian Pharaoh, played by Yul Brynner turns to Moses (Charlton Heston) and says, "When I saw the water turn red, at first I too was afraid. Then I learned of magicians who mixed clay with the water to turn it red." Here was the invisible, proud Pharaoh willing to disclose a personal side of himself in front of his men, ". . . I too was afraid." Whether the Pharaoh was a good leader or not, his openness and willingness to reveal himself in the face of this showdown was notable. My hat is off to the script writer for including this important self-disclosure into the dialogue.

ACCEPTANCE

Acceptance is allowing others to be where they are and not necessarily where you want them to be. It, too, requires a lack of value-judging. It begins with self-acceptance, because only from self-acceptance can you truly accept other people and their differences. By accepting yourself with all your faults and limitations, foibles and frailties, you also are setting the stage for others to accept you more readily.

You are not perfect. No human being is. You face challenges, just like your employees do. Your conclusions about certain topics are not always fixed. You have your share of doubts, uncertainties, and frustrations. You are not there to be God, or to be macho. Your task is to do the best job you can do, and in the broader context, solve problems. Ideally, you are the resource person for followers seeking what steps to take next.

You are an idea generator, a benign influencer, and someone to count on.

ACCEPTANCE BEYOND THE SELF

Can you both accept yourself and accept the individual characteristics, traits, skills and idiosyncrasies of your followers? Like you, they are not perfect—they have strengths, weaknesses, and preconceived notions. The effective leader meets the followers in their camp and sits around their campfire. To influence by design, go where they are, instead of insisting that they come to you.

As we saw in the first two chapters, they come from a variety of backgrounds, applying what they know to do their work. At any given moment, on any given task, they are doing the best they can do, even if they totally mess up, for in a metaphysical sense, if they could do better at that moment, they would.

As a result of accepting yourself as you are, several things happen. The followers feel your acceptance and begin to be more self-accepting themselves. As a result, this makes them more open to accepting your guidance and direction, irrespective of their backgrounds. This upward spiral of mutual acceptance leads to enhanced capability on the part of your followers to accept criticism and re-direction. They are less likely to take criticism personally and attach extraneous meaning to it. They are able to accept other team members more readily, too.

CONGRUENCE

Congruence, a word not used by many people, is most easily described as occurring when the words and the music match. Congruence means you walk your talk. Your behavior is in alignment with what you preach. If you believe in honesty, you have to display honesty. On each and every encounter with followers, you have to be honest. Otherwise, you are issuing platitudes.

As a leader interested in building trust you have to examine what you are transmitting to ensure that your actions are congruent with your statements. It's not always easy to do, and few of us want to be held accountable for everything we say. Yet, to build trust as a leader you have to maintain congruence. Do you use the words *teamwork* or *team-spirit* but don't exhibit any yourself?

If you merely utter the terms, but don't live them, your words ring hollow. You are better off, literally, not using them at all. If you talk about fairness, but you treat one employee one way and another another way, eventually all employees suspect just how fair you are. Then, every time you bring up the term, they will wonder what you really mean by it.

Bill Arnold is the president of Centennial Medical Center, a large HCA hospital in Nashville. He's a forward-thinking executive who strongly advocates open communication with all team members. He encourages and supports the "open door policy" and to show how serious he was about his own communication, he literally removed the door to his office and replaced his desk with a table. His behavior matches his verbal and written communication that says, "I am available."

INTEGRITY

Integrity, or credibility, means doing what we say we are going to do when we say we are going to do it. It is making promises that are kept, and are not over-promising. It is maintaining fairness and consistency to all. It is not just giving team members information, but further explaining how it fits, what we are going to do with it, what your role is. It is giving them the big picture and then elaborating on how all the pieces fit.

A few years ago, the Johnson & Johnson company experienced what might have been a knockout punch to other companies. Someone was tampering with their product Tylenol, lacing tablets with cyanide and several consumers died as a result of ingesting Tylenol.

When the product tampering first made the nightly news, employees throughout the company were profoundly unnerved. The immediate conclusion and fear was that someone within the company was responsible for product tampering, or worse, the problem was widespread. It was not easy for thousands of employees to come home to their communities at night and face neighbors and friends who wanted to know what was happening and why.

Strong leadership at Johnson & Johnson rose to meet a challenge that could have dramatically eroded the long-term market share of not only Tylenol, but the company's entire product line. Though it was found that the problem was not caused by the company, the company chose to engender trust both internally and externally by taking immediate steps which conveyed integrity. A long-time class act in its industry, Johnson & Johnson decided to pull the product from shelves nationwide at considerable loss to the company, and at the same time *not* emphasize that FBI investigations had concluded that the company was not at fault.

The company's bold, swift, decisive action won them favor with the consuming public, the media, the business press, and investors and analysts throughout the world. As a result, the incident is a largely forgotten, undesirable aspect of the company's history, while the corporation itself has been able to build strong customer loyalty, solid growth, increased stock share, and a worldwide reputation for integrity.

INTEGRITY IS KEEPING PROMISES

Integrity is moral and intellectual honesty. Doing what you say you are going to do. It is everything from returning memos and phone calls to taking time for your staff. In simplest terms it is following up on the promises you make, no matter how small.

I am amazed at the number of people who say, "I'll get back to you," or, "I will give you a call," when they have no intention of doing that. Why do they say it? It's safer than engaging in a diatribe about why they won't. Many people are afraid to say, "No I'm not going to call." So, rather than reject, they offer what they see as a meaningless, minor promise. What they don't understand is that *to the person who will be waiting for your call, a promise has been broken.*

There is long-term damage to your ability to influence your followers by design when you say, "I will get back to you," and you have no intention of doing so. People begin to discount what you tell them. "Well, he never returns phone calls." Many people counter with the argument, "I am pressed for time, and I don't see the necessity of returning all phone calls or responding to all messages."

Let's explore what happens when you do return all calls. Denis Quinlan is the Vice President of Human Resources at Alliant Health Systems (profiled in the next chapter). Usually, I don't leave phone messages when I call people because my experience has been that they simply don't return calls. However, I know when I call Denis and leave a message, he is one of the few people who will make the return call. Denis is so prompt and so forthright in his handling of messages that I will never abuse this relationship.

One day, I left a message for him to call me back. A few minutes before five the phone rang and I knew it was him. I said, "Denis, you are one of the few executives I can always count on to return calls." He responded, "I just think it's the mark of a professional." Denis knows that there is a person behind each message on an answering machine or in a voice box. As he rose in his career, like most people, he experienced the false promises of those who never returned messages. Most likely he vowed that when he became an executive he would not act that way. As a result, if Denis leaves a message for me, I will move heaven and earth to get back to him as soon as possible, and I suspect others feel the same way about him.

What about the people who call who genuinely are wasting your time? What if you don't have the luxury of being able to call back as you would like to? We all get telephone calls from brokers, financial planners and the like, in addition to calls that come as a result of our primary business activities. I say be forthright and be brief, but return the call.

FIND A WAY

Bruce Bastian, Chairman of the Board of the WordPerfect Corporation, is a leader who also practices high integrity in terms of getting back in touch with people. In the late 1970s, during the company's formative years, he was never too busy to return calls, and was specific and helpful in answering questions.

There are many things that we can learn from Bastian, not the least of which was the indefatigable way he went about asking others how his software program could be improved. A hardworking, energetic leader, Bastian instilled in employees the importance of listening to the customer. Today, WordPerfect is perhaps the leading word processing program available. The software works with more printers than any other software around. The company is continually making improvements based on the feedback they get from users.

Although many companies maintain an open, cooperative atmosphere, the WordPerfect Corporation does so with a consistency that is a marvel to behold. Bastian engendered trust in his employees, and they in turn helped customers to engender trust in the company.

If one of your *staff members leaves a message or memo that says he needs help, I implore you to respond as quickly as possible.* I see it as a mandatory aspect of leadership and of demonstrating integrity. If you find yourself continually unable to respond to your staff's messages in a timely manner, then I suggest you re-arrange your schedule or build into it time to adequately respond to each follower's needs.

Don't say, "I will get back to you" if you won't. Don't say, "I will take care of it" if you can't. If you are over-committed, or your schedule simply doesn't allow it, help them to figure out a way to accomplish what they are trying to accomplish without you being there. Or, tell them *when* you will get back to them and *then get back to them, precisely at that time.* It may not be at the time they wanted you to respond, but it most definitely is a time in which *you will* respond, and that's something they can count on.

Reorienting Your Staff

8

> *You cannot teach a person anything.*
> *You can only help him discover*
> *it within himself.*
>
> **Galileo**

Unless you are beginning a new organization from scratch, or have newly-acquired leadership status, the odds are you will be working with existing followers. No matter how many changes you make in *your* leadership style, obviously others are not going to change overnight. In addition to building trust, to empowering an existing staff, and to becoming more effective at influencing by design, on some level, you will need to reorient your current staff. Your goal becomes one of developing more empowered, more effective followers, who can more readily accept and support your vision and mission.

I believe you can't solve today's problems with yesterday's ideas and that by empowering others you find new ways to create effective solutions. In his book, *The Service Edge*, Ron Zemke says that to be empowered, employees/followers need **information, resources** and **support.** To reorient your staff, to better prepare them to handle change, you need to be able to provide these items, and your followers need to be able to accept them.

INFORMATION

No one works well without adequate information. One of your chief responsibilities as a leader is to constantly ensure that your followers have the information, data, or facts they need to do their jobs. I know many leaders who are always clipping articles, and information and making sure that they are circulated to their staffs. Not giving followers the information they need to accomplish a task or complete a project is tantamount to wasting their time and talents.

RESOURCES

The second component of empowerment, fundamental for reorienting your staff, is to provide appropriate resources. Resources are often money, but that's not the whole story. Many times resources entail specific training to move from A to B successfully. Leaders skilled at influencing by design build into the reorientation process enough time and reinforcement so that followers may learn new skills or acquire new habits in support of where the organization is now heading.

Offering appropriate resources assumes increasing importance as the change increases. If one of your followers successfully came through a transition period three months before, it is all the more important that you lead the person through another transition period with understanding and care.

SUPPORT

Support is a critical component for reorienting your staff. The effective leader understands that to successfully guide followers through change requires continuous support. Major change simply doesn't take place in one day, a week, or even a month. There will be lingering questions, concerns, and doubts on the part of employees. An effective support system is one that recognizes that employees will have questions one, three, maybe even six months from when the changes were first introduced.

Any employee, no matter how secure, and no matter how long with the company, always has the same question when change is introduced: How will this affect me? How will this affect what I do? To the best of his or her ability, the leader skilled at influencing by design anticipates the questions and concerns that staff people may have.

CARE AND FEEDING

Frequently information, resources, and support are best offered in unison. The president of one company goes so far as to schedule small group meetings throughout the week so that in the course of a month he meets with all of the 220 employees in the company. At another company, questions are anticipated in advance, printed on a question-and-answer sheet and circulated to all staff. On the last page of the question-and-answer sheet, in bold letters employees are encouraged to bring any other questions they have to one of several "transition leaders."

At yet another company, top executives make the rounds on a regular basis. Staff members at all levels know that the top executives understand and appreciate the changes the staff is going through, and that top management is with them all the way, not just in words, but in deeds.

In reorienting your staff, here are some other suggestions for demonstrating your support:

- Prepare a series of memos, perhaps in different colors, to be dispensed on a frequent basis. Each memo addresses some vital component of the change being introduced.
- Offer Friday afternoon, "get it off your shoulders" discussions where employees are encouraged individually, and in small groups, or department-wide to express their frustrations, concerns, and challenges.
- Set up an answer desk, or internal hotline phone for the purpose of responding to transition-related questions.
- Produce an audio or video tape, or tape series with the president or division head directly communicating to team members.
- Schedule organization or department retreats away from phones, computers, fax machines, and other disturbances to get at the heart of issues concerning team members.

The challenge in offering information, resources, and especially support, is that often you cannot put a time frame on them. People feel comfortable about change at varying rates. Some, unfortunately may not be able to make the transition. Others will make it but begin to slip back to old ways of doing things.

Many followers will be afraid to bring up concerns or ask questions. Some silently harbor the notion, "I'm the only one who doesn't understand." Even when it may not apparently be needed, your job is to keep asking questions. Draw out concerns of employees who might not otherwise respond.

- How are you feeling today?
- How are last month's changes working out?
- What challenges are you facing right now?

A COMFORTABLE TRANSITION

One organization in West Virginia is currently experiencing rapid growth. The president of the company never had an administrative assistant, though the need was apparent. In consultation, we decided that the receptionist was most qualified to move into the post of administrative assistant. While she is learning the responsibilities of the new post, she also has responsibility for training her replacement.

During this transition phase she needs to recreate her relationship with the president of the company from that of receptionist to administrative assistant. The president, in turn, is charged *with empowering her with information, resources and support such that she knows she can do the job.*

The key to the receptionist's effective transition to administrative assistant is having an optimal amount of time built into the plan. She must not feel rushed and pressured, but be given the opportunity to aspire to the responsibilities and duties of the new position in the manner that best serves her and the president in the long term.

Once she trains her replacement at the receptionist desk, her role as administrative assistant will expand. Rather than introduce all of her new responsibilities at once, the president of the company will be a more effective leader by pacing this reorientation process.

ALL IN DUE TIME

Applied to your setting, any time new responsibilities or equipment are introduced to employees, a component has to be built into the equation to give them the necessary time and resources to become fully immersed in those new responsibilities or at mastering that new equipment. It is not enough to simply offer a two- or three-hour training program and then leave the employee in the lurch. Training and follow-up are necessary, perhaps followed by more training.

As leader you are charged with the responsibility to understand how the follower feels about the change. Get him talking, to express fears and concerns, breakthroughs and victories. To soften the impact of rapid change on your follower from the outset, convey the message that he is not required to learn the new information or system on his own time.

With any reorientation process, if you only look at the short-term benefits, you are liable to get anxious about costs and how much time it is taking. When you don't look at the long-term, it's easy to get overly concerned about the two or three hours of work each day that isn't being accomplished during the transition phase. Both leader and follower are apt to get more frustrated.

You may feel the urge to foist more of the learning responsibilities onto the private hours of the individual follower, and otherwise loyal followers will begin to feel put upon. Have you ever had an otherwise productive employee depart on relatively short notice following some change in responsibilities? If so, it might have been because the person was not given adequate information and the necessary resources to effectively make the transition. Moreover, many departing employees never voice these concerns—they feel a growing sense of frustration and regard leaving the organization as the quickest route to resolution.

When you look at the long term, it is easier to balance long-term benefits to the organization with short-term costs. Too many organizations throughout the U.S. today are short-term focused, particularly in the face of change. Consequently, they jeopardize their long-term competitiveness.

IN LEADERSHIP,
ADAPTIVE SKILLS PREVAIL

Everyone in your company, including you, possesses some blend of three basic skill categories: functional, adaptive and technical. Functional skills, regarded as "I can" skills, include basic management and self-management skills. For example:

- I can plan.
- I can organize.
- I can schedule.
- I can influence.
- I can control.
- I can implement.
- I can evaluate.

Adaptive skills, "I am" skills, represent characteristics of your own personality. For example:

- I am persistent.
- I am energetic.
- I am caring.
- I am forceful.
- I am enthusiastic.
- I am precise.
- I am a great listener.

Adaptive skills are skills that describe you and your personality. Adaptive skills are also known as people skills—how you relate to others.

The last group, technical skills, are the "I know" skills. These are skills that you need to know specifically for your industry or profession. They are reflected in statements such as:

- I know how to use this software program.
- I know how to care for a patient who is on intravenous medication.

- I know how to encourage participation in a small group.
- I know how to use computer-aided design.
- I know how to write a grant.

Functional skills are those that are very specific to a job. Even though two individuals are in the same organization, even in the same department, their functional skills may differ vastly. All three types of skills are important when it comes to achieving, but without adaptive skills, the "I am" skills, you are not likely to progress within your organization or influence others.

Why focus on the distinction between adaptive, functional and technical? *Studies at leading universities indicate that 85% of your success on a job is derived from adaptive skills—your ability to deal with people.* To effectively influence by design, to lead by empowerment, to reorient your staff, to create positive change is more dependent *on how you are with your followers than what you know.*

What your followers learn will be in direct proportion to the effectiveness of your approach with them. How you are with them is far more important than what you tell them. How they accept what you have to say similarly will be in direct proportion to your approach.

REORIENTING PRIORITIES

Ultimately, reorienting your staff also means reorienting your own priorities. When a follower needs help, you may see that as 58th on your list. I say move it up to at least number three. To be a master at influencing by design maybe you need to make it first.

Your goal is to anticipate, not just respond. If you circulate a memo, consider in advance what needs your followers may have as a result of this memo. What is likely to happen? What questions are likely to be asked? I started my career as an operating room nurse, and in that environment, if you don't anticipate what is likely to happen next, you may lose the patient. In advance, you have to know exactly what to hand the surgeon.

What would your ability to lead be like if you made responding to your staff priority one and anticipating their needs a regular exercise? Clearly, it is not a natural inclination. Yet, if your employees are the ones who produce the work that yield sales and profits, your path becomes apparent.

REORIENTATION: A CASE HISTORY

Alliant Health System, headquartered in Louisville, Kentucky has 4,400 employees. While moving to a Total Quality Management culture, and following a merger of two hospital corporations, they also created a one-day program to reorient everyone in the organization. The program guides employees through the organization's new perspective, and gives all employees first-hand information on marketplace trends and the challenges the organization faces.

Drawing upon the president's vision and a well-established mission statement the Alliant program reinforces within employees the goal of achieving a combined hospital system that offers outstanding resources to serve the people in the region.

The Alliant program outlines components of the new system, solicits the support of all employees, and helps define the role of each employee. It is delivered in a supportive atmosphere, with presenters who are eager to answer questions and who recognize that employees have a vested interest in learning all they can about their company.

The Alliant evolutionary approach to reorienting 4,400 people stands as a modern-day model of an organization's ability to impart the level and volume of information necessary to empower its workforce.

WHAT MAKES FOR QUALITY?

The way in which Alliant has been able to institute major organizational change among an existing workforce provides an example of how any organization can effectively administer training and reorientation programs. The road to reorientation was occasionally rocky, evolving over several years. Today, Alliant is reaping the rewards of their innovative efforts.

Bill Newkirk is Alliant's director of education and training with responsibility for education of managers as well as staff professionals and non-professional employees. "In the hospital business, quality is the competitive edge," says Newkirk. "This was first recognized by one of Alliant's forefathers, James Petersdorf. He began investigating what made for high-quality service some 23 years ago when he headed NKC Hospitals, which later became a component in Alliant Health System.

In 1985, Petersdorf commissioned a team to scour the country to see what made for a high-quality service offering. This team visited Stew Leonard's Dairy, Tom Peter's Skunk Camp, Florida Power and Light, Crosby's, McDonald's Hamburger University, and many other places. When the tour was completed, the group suggested to Petersdorf that they create their own model for total quality management.

From there a quality council was developed with quality committees reporting to it. The various quality committees were assigned the task of quality training, quality education, quality assurance, managers' commitment to quality, customer satisfaction, and so forth. These were ground-breaking activities, as there were no other models for quality health care of this magnitude. Ultimately, the programs were so successful that Alliant won the first annual quality in health care award, The Healthcare Forum WITT Award: Commitment to Quality.

Alliant defined quality as, "meeting the requirements." That meant the customer's requirements. This definition required a clarification of who the customer was. The customer was simply not just the patient or those paying the bill, it was also other entities dependent upon Alliant's work, *i.e.*, physicians, employees, vendors, volunteers, etc. As the Alliant conception of quality emerged, it faced the question, "Can an organization offer outstanding quality and maintain reasonable costs?" Alliant was convinced that the two were compatible.

Customers always expect good value for their health care dollars, technical competence, and service excellence. These three expectations became the guiding principles at Alliant for all health-care employees and managers, with every patient, every day, whether someone is working an eight-hour, 12-hour or 16-hour shift.

Is it a challenge to get every employee to buy into this vision? You bet!

DELIVERING THE MESSAGE OF QUALITY

Each of the three health-care institutions that merged to form Alliant had long been leaders in their respective market niches. The challenges facing the organization necessitated, however, that its level of quality and service be taken to a higher plane which would enable Alliant to maintain its leadership position and continue to attract a wide constituency.

To first offer, and then sustain, an unprecedented level of quality, in 1987 Alliant designed a two-day program for all of its managers starting with senior managers, moving on to various groups by division and department. The objectives were simple—to define quality, communicate why Alliant was placing tremendous focus on quality, convey the benefits to everyone of offering high quality, and impart the reality of rising customer expectations. The program was also designed to convey to attendees the tremendous competitiveness of the health-care industry, and that the long-term reputation of the organization needed to be upheld.

The two day program particularly conveyed to managers that Alliant Health System was indeed a business, and that sound business practices within the context of a health-care institution would help maintain and expand market share, total revenues, and profitability. This was important for them to grasp. Most of them had never been trained in operating a business. They were health-care professionals serving others. Hospitals seemed to run whether anyone paid attention to profitability or not. Now, a new sense of quality and service, mixed with the importance of efficient operations, permeated the air.

One of the tenets of the Alliant quality system was to do the job right the first time. Another was to streamline operations, *i.e.*, convert a seven-page flow chart to one page. The training program conveyed that by increasing productivity and streamlining procedures, everyone would be more satisfied, more productive and costs would actually go down.

The program emphasized the fact that the other people wanted Alliant's market share and were taking vigorous steps to be successful in this quest. To this day, Alliant managers get quarterly information on the corporation's market share and monthly budget information. Managers then, in turn, share this information with their staffs.

A FALSE START

In early 1989, Alliant embarked upon an ambitious program of orienting all of its employees. The program, which took four months, delivered the same message that managers had been exposed to earlier. A train-the-trainer approach was employed— managers who had already attended the program on quality, attended new sessions where *they would learn how to convey the quality message to their staffs.*

Alliant felt that it did not have time or resources to offer a centralized training program and assumed that managers taking the train-the-trainer program could impart the proper message. It didn't happen. Alliant's top-down approach didn't enable the front-line workers to feel as if they had had a hand in the program. Many workers felt disenfranchised. They were told that quality would have to be upgraded and they were given a variety of new forms and data sheets to complete. Barriers between management and staff went up almost immediately. Employees felt as if quality would hang them, and that they would suffocate under the new reporting requirements.

From this lesson, Alliant learned that quality had to be generated on the front line, from the people involved in the day-to-day operation of the organization. The front-line worker had *to want* to change things for the customer.

INFORMING, STORMING, NORMING AND PERFORMING

As the process of informing wore on, Alliant experienced its share of storming—resistance from employees. Eventually, the organization saw this as healthy. The quality teams began to hear that troops were not rejecting the idea of quality, only the way that it had been forced into their lives. Over time, reporting requirements and other paperwork was reduced. Managers began collaborating more with their staffs to achieve true quality improvement.

The process moved from storming to norming—standards were established by managers and employees alike. There were still weak spots and barriers, but slowly those began to dissipate as performance levels edged upward.

WHAT ABOUT NEW EMPLOYEES?

In mid-1989 Methodist Evangelical Hospital merged with NKC, Inc. to form Alliant. The quality education and training committee held the view that for Alliant to maintain a high-quality posture across the board, it would have to ensure that new divisions and new employees brought on be exposed immediately to the vision of quality health care.

The education and training committee developed a one-and-a half-day mandatory orientation program for all new staff, *to be attended before ever assuming a work station.* The orientation included the history of the organization, its products and services, a definition and description of its customers, customer service requirements, quality concepts, plus a tour of the organization, and a meeting with key executives and department heads.

The manner in which this orientation program evolved merits recounting here. At an executive retreat, Bill Newkirk met with senior managers to discuss what to include in the orientation program. "Instead of trying to accomplish the impossible," he said, "you reverse the question and ask senior managers what they felt was important."

Turning on mood music and leading the managers through guided imagery, Newkirk asked penetrating, revealing questions about what they wanted for their new employees, such as:

How would the new employees get to the parking lot?
How would they feel when they got there?
How would they find the education and training room?
What does it look like?
Who is there to greet them?
What will the curriculum be?
What do they need to know?
Who will they eat lunch with?
Where will the managers eat lunch?
How long will the sessions be?
How will they become familiar with the organization?
How will they become familiar with the various departments within the organization?

At the end of this guided imagery session, Newkirk passed out a piece of paper and asked each person to write down everything he could recall from the guided imagery. He posted all of the pages on the wall and said, "During the next two days if there is anything else you think of, please add it."

At the end of two days, the papers were collected and given to the education and training committee who were told how these pages had been created. From there, the committee was able to design an orientation that has proven to be extremely effective. Since its origin, the program has been expanded to two full days.

AN INDELIBLE IMPRESSION

"When the new staff members come out of the orientation," says Newkirk, "they have great pride and enthusiasm for their new organization." However, would program attendees— people new to Alliant—continue to maintain enthusiasm as they confronted the reality of daily operations? Would their pride stay strong working side-by-side with other people who might be suffering from hardening of the attitude?

One year and counting, the enthusiasm has held. More than 1,600 new people attended the orientation program before reporting to their work stations, and their overall impact on the organization has been magnificent. Think of it—15 to 20 super-charged people coming into your organization every other week. It makes an impact. At Alliant, new employees enter from the ranks of student nurses, all the way up to mid-level managers. Even summer interns are required to attend the two-day orientation program.

As Alliant Senior VP Steve Williams says, "We need people who can grow into our system. We want people who are able, willing, enthusiastic, committed and confident to make decisions for customers on the spot that relate to values, technical quality, and customer service."

"The importance of the training cannot be underestimated," adds Newkirk. "One inappropriate remark to a customer can cost you a million dollars. One mistake on the part of a physician can cost millions of dollars. To me, the orientation program is the third step of the empowerment process. First you have to have a vision and a commitment to that vision. Next, you have to select people who have high potential to render effective service to customers—the way we want to serve customers. Then, you have to orient them in a way that leaves a lasting, positive effect."

START BY THINKING

As opposed to filling orientation time with activities, the program encourages new employees to think right from the start and to focus on desirable outcomes and how to measure them. Newkirk says, "We get the new employees interested in knowing how they can *prevent* having the customer return."

"We talk about achieving total customer delight—the phrase 'customer satisfaction' has been abandoned, because it simply is not enough. We show each new employee how outcomes can be measured, and how we use the data to maintain and enhance our overall quality level. We show them typical reports and data using high-quality presentation graphics. We go on to discuss treatment, the outcome of treatment, and how it can be measured.

"If the new employee can come out of the orientation understanding that there is only one reason why Alliant is in business, to serve the customer, then the program has worked. Their reason for being with us is not for the company to earn dollars—a by-product that will occur if everything else is in place.

"Making dollars for the corporation is not a very motivating concept," says Newkirk. "Likewise, they are not with us for their family, community, God, the government or anyone else, except the customer. It is a very exciting concept when framed in those terms."

REORIENTING EXISTING STAFF

In late 1989, a new employee at Alliant attended the orientation program. He then went on the road for two weeks for additional training, where he discovered that some of the Alliant veteran staff he was working with didn't know what he knew. This employee suggested that all employees attend a yearly reorientation program. The idea took hold.

In January 1990, recognizing that some veteran workers did not know what newly-oriented employees knew, and as the corporation was merging with two other hospitals, Alliant introduced an annual *reorientation* program which became mandatory for all employees. The program had the strong support and enthusiasm of G. Rodney Wolford, CEO and President.

Over four months, 2,800 people were reoriented—it was an enormous task. The program, entitled "Welcome to Health Care," accommodated 100 people and consisted of a one-day session which required that attendees sit all day long. Especially for veteran Alliant employees, one day proved to be too long a stretch. Also many of the segments in the orientation program didn't need to be included.

While initially the programs ran from 8:30 to 4:30, they were streamlined to 8:30 to 3:30. Sessions enabled attendees to capture the magnitude of the Alliant Health System and to personally feel their part in it. They gained a first-hand understanding that any interaction they have in the system interacts with other parts of the system. Along the way, there were other rough points, to be sure. As a result of each session, more was learned and instituted in time for the next scheduled session.

EMPHASIS ON OUTCOMES

The sessions were filled on a registration basis. Employees filled out a brief form indicating which date of several dates could best accommodate them. When a session was filled, alternative choices were selected. A single session might contain managers, clerical workers, health-care workers, senior staff, interns and a wide variety of other employees at various levels throughout the organization. It didn't matter that the groups were mixed. In fact, it was a benefit to create a stronger sense of team spirit, and the information that they needed to hear and be exposed to was the same.

The program started much the same as the orientation program, emphasizing outcomes as opposed to tasks. It highlighted the changing nature of health care and the highly-competitive environment. After a few such sessions it became clear that Alliant's real task was providing a basic education about the business of health care, because attendees simply didn't have knowledge of the fundamentals and had no idea about the organization's market share, even though managers had been trained to impart this type of information.

New employees were greeted before the session and requested to sign Alliant's quality commitment agreement. "Maybe this is a form of coercion and maybe it isn't," says Newkirk, "but those who understand and buy into the system tend to do an outstanding job. Those who don't understand and can't buy in are probably better suited for employment elsewhere."

Next, all participants would introduce themselves, which was very appealing to the attendees. They got to know and hear from others in a way that they seldom were able to. Then, all attendees were treated to the "Welcome to Health Care Lecture" with the instructor employing chart pads, slides, video, and other tools.

All the while the emphasis remained not on handling a task or fulfilling a job description but on *achieving outcomes*. The group was encouraged to interact and ask lots of questions. Instructors themselves deliberately asked questions that provoked wide-ranging discussions. For example: "When you go to a service station and someone comes out and washes your car windows why do they do it? Respondents often say, "Because it's his job," or "It's for good public relations."

Does the window care that it is dirty? No.

Does the driver? Yes.

Invariably, the discussion moves to the view that the attendant washes your window because it is dirty and so that you can see out of it effectively. The outcome of this encounter is to have the customer have clear vision through the windshield. In health care, Alliant stresses, "we want to give a good assessment of a patient situation. We want the patient and the patient's family to have a clear idea of what is needed."

As the sessions developed, Alliant developed and streamlined diagnostic tools which provided attendees a way of scoring themselves in key skill areas such as customer service, using the telephone and so forth. Participants enjoyed these types of tools. After all, who doesn't like to learn more about themselves and increase skill areas at the same time?

THE VPS GET "REORIENTED"

Part of the program involved having the corporate vice-presidents speak to attendees on quality. The goal was to have the VPs be visible and communicative. Some proved to be very energetic, enthusiastic presenters. Others simply read the script, word for word and pushed the slide buttons, so Alliant developed an evaluation system whereby presenters would immediately get feedback as to how effective they were with the troops.

Eventually, this type of data was used to ensure that the orientation, reorientation, and any other type of training programs, consistently met high standards. Some of the vice-presidents didn't want to be evaluated, particularly those who bombed. The evaluations were used not to belittle anyone's performance but as an indicator of areas of opportunity.

Alliant provided coaching for VPs who scored low. VPs who tended to be stiff and formal, loosened up. They threw away the script and got in front of the podium to really interact with the attendees. One of them started his presentation as follows, "I have to tell you, I'm not much of a public speaker but I do believe in doing the best job that I can, and I'm committed to having this organization offer a high level of quality." His evaluation for this presentation indicated a dramatic improvement.

Lunch followed the VPs' presentations. Thereafter, attendees were given a history of the organization via a well-designed slide show and a whirlwind slide "tour" of all the hospitals and facilities in the Alliant Health System. They were also presented with slides on Alliant's various products and services.

The initial presenter for this portion of the program, who consistently scored higher on her evaluations than the VPs, was a clerical worker who had been with the company for 11 years. She was a truly empowered person who had found what she did best. From there, her career began blossoming, and she moved on to become a management trainer in another organization. Alliant still uses her as the "voice" on videos they develop to announce benefit changes.

All the while, participants were encouraged to ask questions, and they did. They asked what the organization owned, what our market share was in particular niches, what competitors were doing, how much revenue the organization generated, and what kind of expenses the organization faced. Employees were given an insider's look at the actual numbers related to profit and loss, and what it took to keep the company profitable. Once gaining this information, many employees became visibly cost-conscious and hence more valuable team members.

As part of the continuing education of employees, each employee now receives information quarterly on market share, revenues and expenses, quality ratings and other indicators.

SELF-MANAGING GROUPS

Recently, Alliant has witnessed the rise of self-managing groups within their organization. When the third-shift lab group lost their manager, no one replaced him. The team had so much experience and commitment, it became apparent that the group did not need a manager. They have been managing themselves and doing an excellent job at it. (More on self-directed workers in Chapter 10.)

The Alliant Environmental Service Group consists largely of non-college graduates who undertake their own scheduling. They know their customers, and they take good care of them, particularly when managers leave them alone. The vision Alliant has is to move more towards self-managed groups. To get to this stage everyone needs reorientation, including veterans.

Alliant doesn't expect its employees to succeed simply because of the reorientation program. The system is a continuing process of managers empowering others, by giving them their own power. This can only work when the managers themselves are self-empowered. Managers have to feel good about themselves and empowering others. Some of the old-line managers are still fearful when it comes to empowering others.

HOW ARE WE DOING?

What kind of responses have these reorientation sessions generated among customers? Ovations, yes, even delight. Headquarters has been collecting unsolicited letters from patients and their families in various hospitals in the system who have offered high praise for the treatment and quality of care received.

In the highly competitive health-care field, to simply maintain market share today, according to many industry experts, is to be doing very well. Overall, since the initial sessions for reorientation, Alliant Health System has experienced a stable pattern in terms of market share.

In July, 1990, in its continuing effort to maintain high quality, Alliant requested that all 4,400 employees sign a statement which says that they understand and support the Alliant vision and mission statement. On balance, Alliant has moved mountains in reorienting thousands of employees.

Finding and Keeping Winners

9

> *The final test of the leader is that he leaves behind him with other men the conviction and the will to carry on.*
>
> **Walter Lippman**

O ne of the most effective and powerful strategies available for leading effectively is to hire or attract followers who can support what you're trying to accomplish. This chapter will lay some guidelines for finding and keeping winners. Winners, as used here, will simply mean those people who can be happy, productive, supportive members of your team.

QUESTIONS TO ASK YOURSELF BEFORE YOU TALK TO OTHERS

The best way to ensure a quality staff is to select quality people, yet far too much hiring is done without proper forethought. The U.S. Labor Department says that only about 50% of newly-hired employees last more than six months in their jobs; an obviously poor return on investment. If the wrong person is selected for a job, productivity in that job is likely to suffer, regardless of whatever efforts you or the employee make. In fact, a poor selection will have a negative effect on whatever or whomever it touches.

If you are under-staffed or facing a crunch, and you need a warm body (or warm bodies) quickly, before sending out an all-points bulletin here are several steps that will help to ensure that you find the right person for your department.

First, take out your vision and mission statements. How is your organization or department doing in the context of them?

What do you envision for the new team member?

What are your expectations for the winner to be found?

Will he be on board for the long run?

Why will she want to work with you?

What are the *what's in it for me* factors for the winner you will attract?

In other words, what are the pros and cons—the good news and the bad news—of including this potential player in your company's lineup?

The Good News	Not-So-Good News
•	•
•	•
•	•

While the position is still vacant, form a clear description of the tasks and duties required. What tools, equipment, and support will this person need? How much of it is already in place, how much needs to be acquired? Then, consider the qualities that the applicant needs to perform well on the job. What credentials, experience, skills, talents, aptitudes and interests will increase the probability of a successful placement?

While most leaders/managers do a decent job of describing the ideal candidate, it is also important to know what you are willing to accept as minimal requirements. Remember, no one is going to score 100 percent, across the board, in all the areas you feel are important. Therefore, decide in advance what is acceptable and what is not in each of the areas you have determined is important to fill the position successfully.

After considering such items as salary range and benefits to be offered, your last task before initiating the search is to decide how you will get the job done while the position is open. This is important for several reasons:

- You may not fill the position as quickly as you would like, but work still needs to be accomplished.
- The winning candidate may not be able to join you as quickly as you would like.
- You want to have clear contingencies if the candidate search goes on longer than you anticipated so that you don't resort to panic hiring.

EXAMPLE—
IDENTIFYING THE MANAGER
IN INSURANCE

Let's assume that you operate a claims processing division in a large insurance firm that has a position open for a department manager.

First, determine what the person's tasks are on the job, being as specific as possible with individual duties. This area answers not only what the person is supposed to do but also how the job is best done. If possible, indicate the number of employees for whom he or she would be responsible.

Decide what will enable the candidate to perform the job adequately by considering any job-related skills and experience, intelligence and aptitude, personality characteristics, and attitudes. Often, these related skills are more important than technical skills. It is more difficult to change behavior than it is to teach skills.

Find out as much as possible about the candidate's background. Begin with a thorough review of the application, noting gaps in background information, inconsistencies in the way the application is filled out, and underlying attitudes that reflect reasons for leaving past jobs.

Also, consider how the applicant completes the form. If responses are unclear, ask yourself how this manager might communicate in other situations.

Next, check references, and do it yourself. Start with the candidate list but include related references of employers or people who may know the candidate and his or her past behavior, both personally and professionally. Conclude the background check by interviewing the person extensively. Have a list of questions prepared, observe his or her body language, and listen well. Frequently, much more can be learned from what the person is not saying.

Determine to what extent the candidate possesses or lacks the necessary characteristics, skills, and abilities. Finally, make the decision based on a comparison of all candidates by designing a simple form to help compare them against each other's and management's needs.

WHERE TO FIND CONFIDENT, DEDICATED PEOPLE

Here are several places to look:

Look within your current staff—Sometimes the right candidate is already within your range, but no one notices. It's unfortunate and costly when someone is hired anew to fill a role that could ably be filled by someone already in your company.

Solicit word of mouth referrals—As in advertising, sometimes the best information comes from a tip or referral from people you already know. Consider clients, suppliers, creditors, industry peers and colleagues as possible sources.

Consider offering incentives to your current staff to recruit. Everyone knows at least 10 to 15 other people and employment surveys show that many of the management-level positions continue to be filled by someone in the company recommending someone outside the company.

Review your back pool of job applicants. Often, someone who applied for a previous position may be just the right person for the new position. Sometimes the timing was wrong when interviewing someone, and now the timing may be right.

Advertise in the newspaper. You are likely to get far more resumes than you care to, and many of them will be way off the mark. Happily, a few gems also will arrive.

Use personnel agencies and head-hunter firms. The reputable firms do a good job, though they charge a healthy fee. Depending on your needs and resources, the cost may be worthwhile.

Conduct your own public relations campaign to attract new recruits as a by-product. By writing articles, speaking at job fairs around your community, and visiting the universities, colleges, vocational schools and professional clubs, you can quickly attract motivated applicants for entry-level work.

Set up an intern program—Many organizations get a first-hand look at their future staff members by hiring them as summer interns. Contact the job placement offices of the universities in your area to get involved in these programs.

INTERVIEWING SUCCESS FACTORS

One of the most important keys to interviewing is preparation. Still, this is the one area that many otherwise effective leaders tend to short change. The lack of preparation leads to two major interviewing flaws:

1. Too much talking on your part.
2. Ineffective questioning which gets answers that don't reveal what you need to know to successfully fill the position.

You want to hire the best, so give them your best. Take time to study an applicant's cover letter, resume and anything else submitted. When the candidate arrives, establish a rapport to make him/her feel important. The ideal encounter is *when both parties are looking to buy*—when both are asking penetrating questions, making important observations, and undergoing careful consideration.

Less than ideal is when both parties are attempting to sell one another without offering an accurate, revealing portrait of their needs, wants, desires, strengths, and weaknesses. Ask yourself, can you effectively describe the negative aspects of the position? If not, it is going to be difficult to find the right person and to effectively influence by design.

During the interview avoid letting feelings take precedence over facts. Also, don't make decisions prematurely. The right candidate will still be the right candidate after the second or third time you speak to him.

QUESTIONS FOR EFFECTIVE INTERVIEWING

Based on hiring laws, you can't ask questions on several topics, so let's get them out of the way: You can't ask about age, religion, family status, or finances. Avoid asking about handicaps unless they are pertinent to the job. Don't ask if someone has a criminal record, although you can ask if they have ever been convicted. The main point is: Avoid the appearance of bias in all recruitment and screening.

Your goal is to ask open-ended questions that encourage the candidate to converse freely so that you can gain the kind of information you need to make a wise decision. Here is a roster of open-ended interview questions arranged by categories:

Level and Complexity of Work

In your view, what are the duties and responsibilities of a
_____?
What did your job at _____ consist of?
What kind of decisions did you typically make on that job?
How would you describe a typical day on your job?

Extent of Job Responsibilities

Would you explain just where you fit into the organization?
Would you tell me a little about your boss's job?
How much contact, typically, did you have with your boss?

Motivation

How did you happen to go into that job in the first place?
When did you first think of leaving?
Why did you decide to make a change?
What were some of the things that kept you working at that job?
Describe what you would consider to be the perfect job for you, disregarding any past jobs you've had?

Attitudes and Feelings

What did you like best about the job?
What kind of things didn't you like about the job?
How did you feel about the job, all in all?
What, in the job, did you find particularly satisfying?
How did you feel about your boss?
How did you feel about the company as a whole?
What did you like about the company?
Was there anything about the company or the manner in which they operated that you didn't like or agree with?
Would you describe the kind of company it is?
What kind of atmosphere or climate would you say it has?

How much of a challenge did you find the job? What aspects?

How did you feel about the progress you made?

Effectiveness on the Job

To what extent were you able to increase your earnings between when you started on the job and when you left?

What do you feel were your most significant accomplishments?

What aspects of the job gave you the most trouble?

Why?

How did your boss feel about the kind of job you did?

How do you know this?

Would you describe some particularly tough problems you had to deal with?

How did you make out? How did you tackle these problems?

Major Courses of Study

What subjects did you concentrate on in school?

What were your major and minor areas of emphasis?

What kinds of courses did you take?

Tell me about what you did in school?

Outside Interests

Tell me how you spend your free time?

What sorts of things interest you outside of work?

What kind of free-time activities give you the greatest satisfaction? How did you get interested in that? Have you been interested in that very long?

How would your best friend describe you?

Personal Goals and Objectives

We've been talking quite a bit about your work experience and what you have been doing. Now let's talk a little about the future. Would you tell me what you are looking for in a job change at this time?

What are you aiming toward in the long run . . . let's say 5 to 10 years from now?

If you had a free choice, what requirements would you have in a job that you would like to take now?

What kind of company would you want to work for?

If you could do it all over again, would you still go into the same kind of work? If not, what . . . and why?

Feelings Regarding Your Organization

What do you know about our company?

Why do you think you might like to work here?

CHECKING REFERENCES

Obviously, you are only going to check references for those candidates for whom you have strong interest. Robert Half, in his booklet *How to Check References When References are Hard to Check*, offers the following questionnaire checklist when speaking to references. Note: The telephone conversation is preferable to a written reply since people will offer a variety of vocal and verbal cues:

- How does this person compare to the person who is doing the job now? If you haven't replaced him/her yet, what characteristics will you look for?
- If she was good at her job, why didn't you try to induce her to stay?
- When there was a particularly urgent assignment, what steps did she take to make sure it was done on time?

- None of us is perfect at everything. Please describe her shortcomings.
- Have you seen her current resume? Let me read you the part that describes her job with your company. (Stop at each significant point and ask the reference to comment.)
- She indicated her salary was $24,000 a year. Is that correct? Did that include bonus, overtime, benefits, etc.?
- All employees don't like all other employees. Did she have problems with any type of person in particular?
- How many times a month did she take days off for personal or sickness reasons?
- Did someone refer the candidate to your company? (You want to learn if a relative or client helped her get the job.)
- When she was hired, were her references checked thoroughly? Who checked these references? What did they have to say?

HIRING CANDIDATES AND MAKING A DECISION

Now and then, you get lucky. The best apparent candidate for the job is readily available. When he is not, it's funny how good your second or third choice can look. Often, we become enraptured because a particular candidate is very strong in a couple of key areas. It is more important, however, to weigh all candidates' strengths and limitations versus what you want to have accomplished, how they will interact with the team, what each regards as his best work.

In his hardcover book *Robert Half on Hiring*, the author suggests six ways to increase decision-making success:

- Focus on track record and accomplishments, not just credentials.

- Don't try to force the fit. Turn down what may appear to be the "best" candidate if overqualified by education or experience.
- Put yourself in the candidate's shoes. Be aware of ambitions, commuting time, and career philosophy.
- Give special consideration to motivation, especially when two candidates are relatively equal.
- Limit the number of people involved in the hiring decision or you may get stuck with a "compromise" candidate.
- Don't merely "settle." If you are not satisfied and not desperate, consider alternatives like temporary staffing.

As you go through your evaluation procedure, continually survey your own biases. Attempt to diminish those preferences you may have while accenting total contribution each candidate may potentially make to the team. A key to careful selection is to be cautious. While there is no fool-proof method to guarantee success in hiring, these guidelines will give a much higher return on your initial investment. Your organization will save time, money, and resources by choosing well.

If your interviewing procedure is done with class, your organization's image will gain even from those people who are not selected for employment. Your quest to influence by design extends even to those whom you may not see again. By knowing your needs and wants, your culture and values, with careful preparation, you can increase your chances of adding winners who are in alignment with the organization.

HELPING THE NEW TEAM MEMBER IN MAKING A SUCCESSFUL TRANSITION

The first couple of days and weeks following a new team member's arrival are critical to both her and her long-term contribution. Even the most professional, goal-oriented, self-starting, highly-motivated type of worker needs to know and feel that her arrival has some sense of importance and that planning and forethought have gone into her orientation.

Put the name of the new person on the door. Make sure that her name also appears on interoffice routing forms, and all other files where appropriate.

RETAINING GOOD EMPLOYEES— THE ULTIMATE COST SAVER

A highly cost effective element of leadership is retaining the winning team members. You're already well aware of the cost of turnover, recruitment, orientation and training. When you add it up, keeping whom you have is always smarter.

How do you keep the winners on board? You create a great place to work. Initially, when employees are asked what makes their organization good, some cite attractive benefits. When you probe further, however, you hear words such as trust, pride, freedom, family atmosphere, fairness, and even fun.

In *A Great Place to Work*, Robert Levering says that "good work places seem to share certain qualities." First, they are friendly places. They offer informal, pleasant atmospheres with a relative lack of social hierarchy. Often top executives are addressed by their first names by all employees. Good workplaces also tend to not be too political—there is an absence of constant jockeying for position or having to look over your shoulder. They also treat their employees/followers fairly. Complaints are aired impartially and fully, and resulting action tends to be fair.

Levering also says that great places to work offer more than just a job. Employees have a role in defining what they do and in determining their priorities. They feel that their organization makes a valuable contribution to society and if it's a for-profit corporation, stands for something more than just making money—they are making a contribution. Many employees refer to their organizations as a warm, caring, even intimate organization that treats them much like family.

ADDITIONAL WAYS TO RETAIN VALUED EMPLOYEES/FOLLOWERS

- Help people to feel good about themselves. Maintain your high self-esteem and help them to maintain and build their self-esteem.
- Practice what William McGrane calls TUA—Total Unconditional Acceptance of your followers. On any given day you may not like their behavior, but that doesn't mean that you don't accept them.
- Develop a tuition reimbursement program. Learning is life-long for both you and your followers. Give them the incentive to keep investing in themselves.
- Set the right example by your own actions. You are on stage every second whether you know it or not.
- Communicate expectations—Listen, ask questions, observe, let people in on things, hold regular staff meetings. Consider initiating your own organization or division newsletter.
- Help your followers to define their career paths and as often as possible, promote from within.
- Offer flexible staffing patterns such as job sharing, flextime, alternative work hours and other systems that enable your followers to conduct their careers and personal lives effectively.
- Provide recognition. This could be in the form of "employee of the month" or through bonuses and incentives.
- Provide a safe and attractive working environment. For female employees in particular, ensure that walkways are well-defined, and that lighting and security are more than adequate.
- Be patient and consistent in your own behavior.

- Recognize mistakes—both yours and theirs—as part of learning.
- Foster creativity, responsibility and accountability—that is empowerment at its peak.
- Deliver on promises, no matter how small.
- Maintain fair pay and benefits.
- Reduce social and economic distinctions between management and other employees. If you haven't done so, convert to using first names throughout the organization. Delete special parking and dining for management.
- Use change to break up the mundane routine. Re-design jobs and re-define roles.
- Provide company social times. It may not seem like much, but employees appreciate holiday parties, picnics and occasional office parties.
- Stay flexible! Bend like a willow!

Depending upon your clout within your organization, here are some additional benefits/perks to consider offering to increase the probability of retaining your winners for the long term:

- Offer child care services.
- Set up a credit union.
- Provide investment counseling.
- Award certificates for in-service/education seminars.
- Distribute service pins for long-time employees.
- Devise a transportation program if you have difficulty staffing.
- Establish a fitness/wellness program.
- Introduce a retirement program.
- Grant personal days for staying well.
- Create a mentor program for new staff.

KEEP ANALYZING YOUR SITUATION

Even if you lead with the force of Ghandi, some of your followers will depart for their next challenge. Your role is to do everything you can to retain the winners, if possible. If not, conduct an exit interview to both understand the full reasons why the follower is leaving and to gain valuable information and feedback. People are willing to open up to unprecedented heights when they are about to depart from an organization. The information and insights that you receive from such exit interviews can strengthen your ability as a leader and assist in finding and retaining winners in the future.

Remember, too, that a role of a leader is to develop followers who can move to new positions of leadership themselves. One of the greatest rewards of a leader is to be a part of the advancement of another person's career.

A parting note: Always keep the door open. When a winner is departing, even if she has no thought of reconnecting with your organization at that moment, let her know that if the circumstances for her return ever arise, she would be most welcome. Give her a letter to that effect, because if she ever does seek to reconnect, *you* may have departed by then.

Developing Self-Directed Followers

10

*An individual without information
cannot take responsibility. An
individual who is given information
cannot help but take responsibility.*

Jan Carlzon

Robert Kelley, professor at Carnegie Mellon University, observes that "what American business needs now is more effective followers, not just leaders." You need followers, too, to be an effective leader. The more effective your followers, the more effective your leadership. With flattening organizational structures, downsizing, global competition, and rising costs, developing strong followership is an idea whose time is here.

CULTIVATING EFFECTIVE FOLLOWERS

What does the word followership imply to you? To many people it has passive connotation—sheeplike behavior, moving blindly and doing what you're told. True followership, however, means action, and reflects strength, enthusiasm and self-directiveness. I encourage my clients to teach and model the concept of followership in their own organizations, because successful organizations today need the kind of people who take pride and satisfaction in the role of supporting player.

Followership is a noble
and virtuous pursuit.

Kelley suggests four steps for developing effective followers:

Redefine Terms—Help others to think of leadership and followership as equal though different activities. Followers are capable workers performing vital functions. Convey this view to your followers as you demonstrate your own good followership in situations that call for it.

Hone the Right Skills—Initiate a follower training program that focuses on such topics as improving independent, critical thinking; self-management; and blending personal and organizational goals. Why not gather your team and ask them to define the skills they see as necessary for followership? Ask them what they specifically need from you to build them.

Provide Feedback—Both formally and informally, let your staff know how well they are handling followership roles. Build this into performance evaluations and continually acknowledge those that demonstrate effective followership skills.

Restructure to Encourage Followership—Look at your organization anew, with the ideal of using small task forces that work without supervision; establishing small groups with rotating leadership; delegating to the lowest level to foster increasing responsibility, and rewarding positive followership.

HOW TO BE AN EFFECTIVE FOLLOWER

Most leaders, at some point, are also followers, whether dealing with an outside source, a committee headed by someone else, or superiors within their own organization. As such, here are some guidelines for effective followership, whether coaching your staff, or *serving as a follower yourself:*

- **Give 100 percent support to your leader**—It's easy to focus on another's faults and decide that you won't support him completely because he's not perfect. Cast these feelings aside, and experience what it's like to give someone 100 percent support at the workplace. You may find, as others have, that your ability to offer vigorous support improves in other areas of your life.
- **Strive to make your leader look good to others**—It's very easy to be critical. It's OK to disagree, but do it in private in a direct conversation with your leader. After the meeting or outside the organization, affirm your leader's competencies to others. It does more than make your leader look good. It makes you look good.
- **Communicate openly with your leader**—Listen closely to what your leader has to say, ask for resources and support you need to accomplish your tasks and assigned responsibilities, and openly express your views. A good follower doesn't suffer in silence.
- **Take credit for your successes**—Feel free to toot your horn, when appropriate. No one likes a braggart or someone who is self-aggrandizing. However, many times on the job it's appropriate to gain the recognition and visibility that go with a solid performance. Also, consider that when you take credit for your success, others within your organization, in addition to your leader, have a clearer idea of your capabilities and talents. As such, they may request your services and this may improve your tenure and promotability within your company.
- **Subordinate yourself for the good of the team**—Conversely, in some situations such as when a team member comes up with a great idea that saves time or money, it makes sense to let that person lead the project and take credit. When other team members see you giving that

person the leadership role, they have more respect and trust in you. It also spurs them on to voice their ideas.

- **Be forgiving and live in the present**—No one wants to work with someone who is carrying a grudge from what didn't go right yesterday, last week or last year. Effective followers learn to forgive quickly and move on. They realize that others make mistakes, and that *people can change and grow.*
- **Be flexible**—A good follower, like a good leader, understands the dynamics of the rapid pace at which our society is changing. He knows that today, more than ever, the ability to be flexible is a crucial work and life skill. What came before, and how we used to do it may have little or no bearing on what we face tomorrow, and how we are going to handle it.
- **Avoid giving excuses**—Figure out how you can make something happen, rather than why it won't work, which is always an easy way to shirk responsibility. If necessary, give yourself affirmations such as, "I can make this work," or "I can easily handle this."
- **Be nice**—Studies reveal that those who are effective on the job and who get promoted are those who are nice people to be around. Dale Carnegie was right—who likes to be around a grouch, a doom-and-gloomer, a perfectionist or a complainer? A positive attitude, thoughtful behavior and a sense of humor go a long way in both followership and leadership.
- **Take responsibility for your errors**—Everybody makes errors and high achievers probably make more than their share. When you take responsibility for your errors you open up an effective communication channel and establish a higher level of trust with your leader than is otherwise likely to develop (see Chapter 7).

Jeff Davidson, author of *Blow Your Own Horn: How to Market Yourself and Your Career* and more than a dozen other books on marketing and career development, recalls a time early in his career when taking responsibility for an error turned out for the best. He had goofed royally, misreading the due date for three proposals he was working on for his firm, and consequently couldn't submit any of them.

He walked into his boss's office expecting to be fired, only to be told that, "everybody makes mistakes," and "our winning percentage rate for proposals isn't high enough to worry about it anyway." Weeks later, he was able to convert one of the proposals and submit it elsewhere, ultimately winning a contract award five times the size of the initial quest. Within two months, to Davidson's joy he received a mega-raise.

As you help to encourage effective followership, you foster opportunities for some staff members to become self-directed workers. Let's see what that's all about.

THE SEEDS OF SELF-DIRECTION

Nancy works for a small advertising agency as a receptionist and all around office helper. Her real desire is to be a writer. Recognizing this situation, Nancy's boss attempts to combine Nancy's administrative functions for which she was hired, with opportunities for Nancy to express herself through writing. Nancy doesn't resist her receptionist/clerical responsibilities, but Nancy's boss has seen that Nancy's true passion is released when she is able to exercise her literary flair.

As often as possible, Nancy's boss gives her assignments such as responding to inquiries and clients, assisting with concept papers and proposals, helping craft company literature, and occasionally, writing articles for publication that help position the company.

When people do their *best work*—what is exciting for them, what they are passionate about, what inspires them, what is easy for them—naturally, they will do a better job. They will do the work more often, more clearly, and have more energy for doing the work. Conversely, when people are doing something that deep down they would rather not be doing, consciously or unconsciously, they simply cannot do as good a job.

HELPING OTHERS TO FIND AND DO THEIR BEST WORK

In helping people do their best work, recognize that most people don't know what they want to do or what they are best at. Effective leaders help followers to better understand themselves their strengths and their weaknesses. These are the kinds of leaders who help others to look at their jobs in a new light, and with a different perspective. This doesn't mean that followers only do the parts of the job they like.

As Scott Peck pointed out, in *The Road Less Travelled*, followers get better at delayed gratification. They do the things that they know they need to do to get the job done. That is the follower's responsibility—to create ways to accomplish the work in accordance with how they like to do it—what gives them zeal and enthusiasm. As followers come to understand what they work best at and quit attempting to be the best at everything, they are more free to be creative in their work. That's when it becomes fun and fulfilling.

When I began my consulting and speaking business in 1981, I was by myself and had to do everything from administrative work and sales to program design and delivery of the services. While I'm really not best at all of those, I created ways to get some jobs done quickly so I could spend more energy doing what I loved. I played mental games with myself and set deadlines and goals and followed Scott Peck's ideas on delayed gratification.

One aspect of my best work is on the platform speaking to groups where my personal energy is unleashed. Another is creating structures and organizing thought. There are other parts of my business that I need to tend to, and I do. Other tasks and responsibilities are important for the business to be successful and while I don't get to do what I am best at all of the time, I create the environment where I get to do it *enough of the time* to feel fulfilled.

So, too, with your followers. If they get to do what they are best at and enjoy doing enough of the time, their maturity, emotional wisdom and sense of responsibility will carry them through the other tasks. Overall, they can be balanced, effective employees. Your goal becomes always looking for ways to help your people use what they identify as their strengths, particularly in ways where they can see the contribution they are making to the finished product or desired end result.

As you continue to communicate your vision to your followers you help them to achieve their own vision of how they would like their environment to be. As they envision their ideal work setting and the contributions they would like to make, they begin to acquire a greater sense of self-directiveness and in that respect, your job becomes somewhat easier. You set the parameters; each follower identifies where and how she can contribute. "This is what I like to do. This is my best work."

LEADERS NEED TO FIND
THEIR BEST WORK, TOO

One of my clients is an engineering firm. It began as a family-owned business many years ago. The current president and vice-president are both part owners. The vice-president is a woman who came into the business after her father, one of the founders, passed away. When she first joined the company, she didn't know much about the business, yet she and the current president initially served as co-presidents.

Though they had different titles, they shared chief responsibility for running the company. This arrangement was confusing both for employees and customers. People didn't know whom to report to or whom to call. I was retained to conduct a team building session with the senior executive staff. During the course of my preliminary research about the organization the issue of co-presidency surfaced immediately.

Originally, I was hired for only one day. Four hours into the program I was finally able to get people to open up and talk. It took so long because there was built-up confusion, no one wanted to risk communication and, there were many hidden agendas. Near the end of this one-day session, I knew we were not going to accomplish our objectives. We needed role clarity before we could get on with procedures, building relationships, and achieving results.

For the first time in my nine years in business, I was forced to say, "We have not accomplished what I promised you. There are some things we need to clarify before you can have the kind of team you are telling me you want." I then met with the two leaders. I guided them through a series of questions to help define their best work. They were finally able to express their ideal role in working in this company.

Then we posed a series of questions to each of the senior managers:

- What is important for you at this point in your career?
- What aspects of the company really excite you?
- What would be your ideal scenario?
- What is the concern to you right now?
- What are you resisting?
- What don't you enjoy doing?
- What in your opinion is your best work?

The vice-president confessed that she was uncomfortable when dealing with the engineers, because she didn't know anything about engineering. As we proceeded through this exercise, each person was able, with help, to articulate his own vision. As a result, the president and vice-president were able to separate their roles, much to the relief of everyone in attendance. From there, we assembled the rest of the organizational structure and went on to building a more solid management team, and a more effective followership.

From my experience with this company and many others, I conclusively learned that when leaders do their best work, they are more likely to influence by design. When they help others to do their best work, they help develop a self-directed work force.

CREATE SELF-DIRECTED FOLLOWERS TO YIELD HIGH RESULTS

Creating a self-directed workforce will soon become imperative in most organizations. It is becoming increasingly difficult for organizations to pay someone a salary to simply come in and do a job. If for no other reason than to maintain global and industry competitiveness, there has to be a higher level of accountability on the part of more followers at more times.

To create a self-directed workforce—employees or followers who maintain their own visions for their careers begin by asking questions like:

- What is important to your career at this point in your life?
- Within this organization (or department), if you could create this job and your existence here, what would it look like?
- If you could design your ideal work day, what would it look like?
- What skills would you like to develop?
- If you could design your own professional development plan what would it include?
- What courses would you like to take?
- What kinds of tasks would you like to tackle?
- What challenges you?
- What would you prefer to avoid?

Once you have the answers from each of your followers, your goal is, to the best of your ability, to create such an environment for each of them. You need to be trustworthy and sufficiently reliable that you can say with conviction:

"I want you to be able to use your strengths in this organization. For me to be successful and for you (the follower{s}) to be successful we have to use the natural strengths and gifts that we have and apply them with passion.

"If you could design your job exactly the way you want it, what precisely would you be doing? Who would you be doing it with? I want you to take two or three weeks and think through this. Then we'll meet and have an in-depth discussion so that both you and I understand your vision completely."

This meeting could be done in a large group or on a one-to-one basis.

When Nancy's boss asked these questions, Nancy's whole demeanor changed. She got excited and spoke without hesitation about what she would like to do. It was at that point that Nancy's boss realized the potential benefits to both Nancy and the company, of giving Nancy more writing assignments.

Enabling each of your followers to find his own vision and perhaps to even develop his own mission statement is a fundamental breakthrough in empowerment and in helping them to do their best work. It requires sitting down with the person in a quiet place, preferably not at a performance appraisal; otherwise, the session may be too emotionally charged.

Then, probe for what the individual really enjoys doing, always keeping in mind that he may not know, or cannot easily recognize it at first. Keep him in conversation. As his speech quickens, and his words begin to flow more freely you are moving closer to identifying what is his best work.

SELF-DIRECTED FOLLOWERS EN MASSE

Some of the most successful companies today in the field of multi-level marketing, including Mary Kay Cosmetics, Amway and Shaklee, have developed self-directed followers in the form of downline marketers who carry the companies' products and message out into the field with vigor and enthusiasm. All corporations, however, can instill in their followers a sense of independence, perseverance, personal commitment, and pride in effort. The payoff to the organization is a significant increase in productivity and followers having ownership of their work.

Following the Followers or Others—Lydia Young is a bright woman in Philadelphia. Once an administrative assistant, she found her best work and is now a successful beauty consultant with Beauty Control Cosmetics. She manages and leads an organization of 90 people in her own division. All of her followers are motivated to work and all see how what they do benefits themselves as well as how it fits in the big picture.

On a monthly basis Lydia meets with everyone in a large group. Throughout the month, she will meet with or talk by phone to her followers, as they need to. She doesn't hover over others. Instead she serves as an ever-ready resource, support center, and coach.

SELF-DIRECTED FOLLOWERS ARE ACCOUNTABLE FOR THEIR WORK

One thing that you can *never* do for self-directed followers, is *their* work. They are completely responsible for what they say they will do, and they enjoy being held accountable. They know that no one is going to pick up the pieces or fill in what they leave out. It's their ballgame, and they intend to win.

While multi-level type systems use monetary rewards and prizes effectively to inspire followers, similar inspiration can be generated in organizations *without* using monetary incentives. Consider Federal Express in Memphis, Tennessee. The company employs a concept called "moments of reality" which is somewhat similar to Jan Carlzon's "moments of truth" at Scandinavian Airlines.

A moment of reality for a Federal Express employee is whenever he encounters a customer on a pick up, delivery, drop off, complaint, or other situation. The Federal Express employee communicating with the customer is empowered with choices and options about what he can do. Such latitude enables him to practice self-directed followership. Rather than having to respond to the customer in some routine or fixed manner, the Federal Express employee is free to choose how he will handle the situation, within appropriate boundaries, and therefore take ownership of his action. By contrast, consider followers who are given written scripts, particularly telemarketers. Following the script is the only option that these particular followers have. If they want to make a change, they have to ask their managers. There is no empowerment in such a system and therefore there is no self-direction. The result is inevitable. Too many of these types of followers offer mundane, predictable, uninspired performances. The company wins by having enough of them make enough contacts so that the numbers pay off, but turnover is high and accountability is practically non-existent.

A CASE HISTORY— SELF-DIRECTED FOLLOWERS

If you are in a situation where you have the opportunity to create a more self-directed workforce, the first step is to ask yourself, is this what I really want? Certainly it is not going to happen overnight and changing the culture of an organization or even department brings new transitional problems.

Non-multilevel organizations can also use the principle of self-directed followers to great advantage by letting workers have a hand in designing their positions around their unique strengths. Let's look at the case of Shawn Kent, part of the professional staff at IMS America, a Philadelphia-based software development firm. Shawn feels self-directed because of the way her boss manages her.

When her boss, Steve, hired her to come on board, he said to Shawn, "Tell me what you do best. What are your strengths?" Shawn told him, and she also told him what she didn't do well.

"I am very creative, and I have lots of ideas. I am not always good at paying attention to detail. For example, I am not a good proofreader." Shawn went on to explain that she came up with ideas easily and then liked to have others join her for follow-up and implementation. Steve and Shawn both agreed that Shawn would function best in a team-like atmosphere where Shawn could both give and receive support. Steve created such a team to take full advantage of Shawn's skills and capabilities.

Shawn is able to flourish in such an environment because she has a pretty clear concept of who she is and what she is able to contribute. When she says she will handle something, it is virtually a guarantee that the task will get done. It may not be exactly the way Steve would have done it, but it gets completed effectively, sometimes beyond everyone's expectations. Shawn trusts Steve because of the way Steve creates the space for Shawn to do what she does best.

Steve also asks other members what they like to do, what they feel their strengths are, what they don't like to do, and what they feel they are not well-suited to do. Then he looks for ways to support the team members based on the input they give him. For example, Mary is very strong on the computer and Barbara has some excellent design skills. The net result is a true team where everyone contributes their best work and produces remarkable outcomes.

As we discussed above, most people really don't know what their best work is. If they do, chances are they've never consciously expressed it. So it becomes your task to help them identify what it is and express it. When Shawn first began working with her teammate Mary, Mary wasn't fully aware of how much she enjoyed working with computers and learning about their capabilities. With Shawn's help, Mary has become the computer whiz kid. Steve's team *has become self-directed due in large part to the way the team members empower each other and to the way Steve gives them the space to do what they are best at.*

Ask each of your followers, "Of the work you do, what is the most fulfilling for you?" As followers submit their lists to you, involve them in opportunities that meet their criteria. In our running example, Barbara knows that Shawn is working on a new software communications training program. She has been supporting Shawn with clippings and tidbits of information whenever she encounters them. She then tells Shawn, "Let me know when it's ready for me, and I will do the editing and follow-up."

Threatening to Some—Creating self-directed followers is a function of your desire. Not all leaders want to create self-directed followers. It can be a little threatening. You will probably have to release some control, and it may not feel comfortable for you at first. You will have to devote extra time and effort, at least in the initial stages, to support your followers in becoming self-directed and in effectively exercising their own power.

UNAVOIDABLE ADJUSTMENTS

In creating self-directed followers, ideally, you would first clearly define the position to be filled before associating it with a particular human being. As we discussed in Chapter 9 on finding winners, it is necessary to hunt for a person who embodies what the position entails. Then, you have executed a sound strategy for developing a self-directed follower and a self-directed workforce. Since in most situations you already have a team in place, your task then is to help your followers make the transition to self-directedness.

You may discover that some of your followers are in the wrong department, because realistically, there may be few opportunities for them to do the kind of work that they do best and that they enjoy doing. If this is the case, don't take it personally. Followers share responsibility for ensuring that they are in a setting which supports their visions of how their job or career can be.

Invariably, not everybody gets everything they want, and unfortunately, some people won't be able to receive even the minimal components of their vision to keep them happy. If so, you commit to helping the followers who don't fit to find positions that meet their strengths. You may have to bring in outside resources, such as a recruiter, to help these people reconnect elsewhere—either within the organization or at other organizations. Outside relocation is probably the worst-case scenario.

In the context of creating self-directed followers, a leader who avoids placing staff where they belong and instead sticks them into positions just because they are present and need employment, will lose credibility.

GROWING YOUR OWN PROFESSIONALS

Companies that practice career-pathing to "grow" their professionals need the opportunity to observe them handle a span of functions. Similarly, those on the career path need to experience many functions to progress. IMS America has created a specific position within the company for executives-in-grooming. For one year, such individuals work in the production department and another year in customer service and then spend additional time in another department.

The company is now exploring having many people at different job levels undergo the same type of rotating assignment experience. Typically, individuals in such a program enjoy working on diverse tasks in diverse settings. Their particular strengths are learning quickly, adapting, and seeing how things can connect from a unique vantage point.

In large organizations there are more opportunities to move people around to enable them to handle their best work. In the smaller organization there are fewer employees, and thus fewer employees who qualify or who can respond to the notion of becoming self-directed followers. Still, with innovation, even smaller organizations can introduce aspects of self-direction.

SELF-DIRECTION IN SMALLER ORGANIZATIONS

In one company, 15 objectives had to be met by a department by the end of the calendar year. Following a rigorous procedure of allocating responsibility and making tradeoffs, each team member focused his attention on completing five of the objectives.

For example, Tom was the best qualified to handle objective #1 and so was given chief responsibility for its accomplishment. Tom also was assigned to a supporting role on four other objectives. Other members of the team were given chief responsibility for accomplishing one or two of the primary objectives and given supporting roles in accomplishing other objectives.

Naturally, assignments for chief responsibility followed from each team member's strengths, interests, and capabilities. One of Linda's responsibilities was to work on a project to develop a management program for supervisors—not one of her favorite tasks. However, she was given the opportunity to institute a training newsletter which greatly interested her. Literally, her boss said "Linda, I have a deal for you, if you will work on . . ."

Within any size company, if you take a given number of objectives and allocate responsibility for completing them to a team that has diverse skills and interests, the probabilities are likely that appropriate tradeoffs can be made where everyone gets to do enough of what they like to do. And that further contributes to the upward spiral of self-direction.

PART IV

ADVANCED TECHNIQUES

In this section we'll examine advanced techniques for influencing by design, including serving as coach to the customer contact team and being more effective in working with professional and clerical staffs. We'll also look at how to make change work for you by acknowledging human resistance to change and helping your followers to deal with it to get to new ground.

Working With the Customer Contact Team

11

*Leadership is the crucial element
in achieving service excellence.*
Karl Albrecht

As a leader you may have responsibility for coordinating the efforts of the sales team and sales support team. In working with different employees or followers with different responsibilities, your job is to respond to each type of group according to its needs. In this chapter we will focus on working with the customer contact team. This involves anyone who interacts with customers or clients on behalf of the organization, including the organization sales staff.

In Chapter 12 we'll focus on working with the professional staff which includes college-educated employees serving as lawyers, accountants, nurses, trainers, and consultants, as well as managers; and the support staff, including anyone involved in reception, clerical, administrative, or other assisting functions.

COACHING THE CUSTOMER
CONTACT TEAM

The sales staff, sales support staff, or any employees who have responsibility for making contact with customers need to have their own vision—which connects with philosophies, values, and culture of the rest of the organization.

You have several duties when it comes to teaching, training, and coaching the customer contact team (we'll use "sales team" or "sales reps" for ease of wording). To be effective, your sales staff requires knowledge of behaviors and strategies, as well as specific interpersonal skills, to close sales. To be effective with the sales staff, you need to assume the role of coach, much like the coaches in sports.

Denny Crum is the winning head coach of the University of Louisville basketball program. They were the NCAA champions in 1981 and 1986, and over the years, more than a dozen of his players have gone to play for professional teams in the National Basketball Association. Denny doesn't actually go out on the floor to take shots, guard the other team, or make rebounds. Rather, he helps create the environment that inspires and invigorates his players to do the best job they can do and to work as a smooth operating team. In short, he does everything short of lacing up sneakers and stepping on the basketball court for the game himself.

Part of Denny's role is to provide information much like a sales manager helps sales representatives. Denny presents product information to his players, in the form of techniques, predesigned plays, and strategy. He provides market data—where the team stands in its conference, and the upcoming challenges. He provides competitor information—videos on opposing teams, and individual players' statistics and analysis.

STRESSING THE FUNDAMENTALS

Sticking with sports analogies a bit longer, during his coaching days with the Green Bay Packers, when his team turned in a poor performance during the first half of a game, and the legendary Vince Lombardi wanted to redirect the team in a hurry, he returned to the fundamentals. Lombardi would hold up a football in the locker room to a silent, watchful team, and begin his halftime discourse by saying, "Gentlemen, this is football." The effective sales coach may offer some sophisticated techniques, but keeps stressing the fundamentals as well.

Whether it is using the telephone or calling on prospects on site, each step of the selling process is viewed as critical. And why not? Today the average on-site visit of an industrial sales representative costs the organization more than $400 when you add up all of the costs that make that visit possible.

The coach creates energy and a vision for the sales team. He maintains an almost omnipresent posture making himself accessible and available to his staff. In turn, the sales rep is responsible for developing strategy for each of his individual accounts. The coach's role is to keep asking questions and guide the reps through the kind of advance preparation they will make for each call—how and when they will make the call, what they will present, how they will follow up, and how they will close.

The coach will use every technique at his disposal to assist the reps to be more effective, including role playing where the coach and the rep alternatively pose as a customer while the other poses as sales rep. The larger the account, the more important role playing becomes. During such a session, the sales coach, posing as the customer, would anticipate the kinds of questions and kinds of situations the sales rep would encounter and introduce them during the role play.

Anticipation is the key word. The successful sales coach knows that for sustained sales success, you can't wing it. The sales coach also walks the sales rep through the possible outcomes as the result of the sales call. Too often, sales reps become routinized in their efforts: they see a customer or prospect, offer a pitch, and depart. They don't pause and consider:

- Why am I here?
- What are the best interests of the customer?
- What am I attempting to accomplish on this call?
- What preparation is needed for me to be effective?
- What message do I want to impart?

All sales calls, obviously, are not alike. Some calls are simply to meet a prospect for the first time. Others are to gather additional information. Especially in the case of sales of high-technology equipment or large-scale machinery, many, many calls may be necessary leading up to a close.

The sales coach understands the sales cycle and is able to impart this to the sales rep. He knows how long it takes on average to close this type of sale. He has a fair idea of the internal decision-making process of various types of prospects and he is able to share this with sales reps *not in the form of lecture or instruction*, but often in the form of questions and comments that come up as a result of his role playing.

COACHES DRAW OUT THE ANSWERS

The best coaches are able to assist their teams in helping prospects find what they are really looking for, *i.e.*, what the prospect really needs. The answer is not always clear. Consider the option in telephone and message systems. The coach helps the sales rep to look at the prospect's business or division analytically, to recognize bottlenecks and pressure points, and to devise creative solutions that address important needs. The coach also helps his followers to become skilled at "people reading," to understand what differences in posture, facial expression and gestures convey.

FIELD TRIPS

The best coaches periodically accompany their sales reps on sales calls. In one insurance agency with which I work, we now have the sales manager accompanying each of the field sales staff two or three times a month. "Isn't this something that a sales manager would do naturally?" Not necessarily. It depends on the company and what other responsibilities the sales manager has. There are few short cuts to being an effective sales coach, however, and the only way to observe a sales rep in action is to actually be there.

Particularly for sales managers who have a large sales staff or too many other responsibilities, it's easy to short-change this crucial aspect of their role. Some coaches only accompany newly hired or poorly performing sales reps, not giving attention to other reps, including successful ones, who need continual coaching. It's a false notion for a coach, or sales rep, for that matter, to believe that adequate or exceptional performers don't need coaching.

In the Olympics, the fastest sprinter, the highest pole vaulter, the gold medal winning backstroker, all have coaches, often train under the watchful eyes of their coaches, attend the Olympics with their coaches, and continually listen to their coaches even between heats. In some organizations, sales managers only see sales reps once a month or once quarterly, not enough to ensure that even successful reps achieve optimal performance.

TEA FOR TWO

While the need for the sales manager to accompany the sales rep is mandatory, the mechanics are to be carefully approached. Two visitors may inadvertently overwhelm a prospect. Nevertheless, when the sales rep is able to bring in her sales manager, it lends status to the call—to both the sales rep and the prospect.

Prior to the call, the coach reminds the sales rep of why they are here calling on this customer and what they hope to accomplish. If the sales coach is doing her job, the sales rep will probably turn in a better-than-average performance because she will be freshly reminded of the purpose and objectives of the call. This immediately eliminates calling on the same prospect every Tuesday because that is the habit that someone fell into.

Sometimes by calling on a prospect less frequently, but more closely aligned to the prospect's needs and rate of decision-making, sales effectiveness can increase vastly. The sales coach who accompanies a sales rep in the field is often able to detect small nuances in a situation, whereas a rep who sees the client more often may miss signals.

Following the introductions, and an exchange of pleasantries, the effective sales coach *says very little for the duration of the sales call*. Her job is to watch closely, listen, make mental notes, and look for opportunities to coach the sales rep at a later time.

DON'T TELL, DEBRIEF

After a sales call, many coaches find it difficult to resist telling team members what they need to do. Indeed, the fact that one became the sales manager may have been due to one's "telling" ability. The better you are at telling, the more you have to work on listening, affirming, and coaching. In essence, you are now selling to your sales reps. You are using effective communications and persuasion skills.

The effective sales coach knows that instead of telling the sales rep what should have or could have been done, there are better ways to coach—such as influencing by design. The most growth-producing approach for the sales rep is not to direct him through instruction, but to ask questions (see next page).

By asking questions, and letting the sales rep respond at length, if necessary, the sales rep is afforded the opportunity to verbalize what he noticed, learned, or may do differently next time. Questions help the sales rep to maintain a higher level of awareness and be more effective with the prospect on the next visit and be more effective on all sales encounters.

The effective sales coach holds back his own observations, making sure that first, he gets the sales rep talking about what the sales rep saw and how he feels. Getting the sales rep talking, the sales coach then asks for permission from the sales rep to provide some pointers to him.

"I have got a couple of suggestions. Are you open to hearing them?" Then, a small switch goes on in the mind of the sales rep, or any customer contact staff person, and he is much more open to new ideas. This is influencing by design at its best. No one likes to be told anything. Referring to the communications skills discussed in Chapter 5, the effective leader does not tell people what to do, he both *models the desired behavior and asks appropriate questions.*

DEBRIEFING ILLUMINATES EVERY ENCOUNTER

When you go through debriefing with a sales rep, you are helping her review what transpired during a sales call in vivid and immediate detail. Here are a variety of questions you can ask to help someone through this process:

- When you asked question XYZ, what were you hoping to gain?
- What was your goal in asking the prospect about ABC?
- Besides what the prospect stated, what else do you think the prospect was concerned about?

- What was the posture or body language of the prospect?
- What, if anything, got him excited?
- Did the prospect seem to be in a hurry?
- What else might you have asked?
- What points did you emphasize?
- How do you think the prospect responded to the details of our service program?
- How were you in responding to his questions?
- What other points would you like to bring up?
- How did your preparation pay off?
- What new things did you learn about the prospect?
- What new things did the prospect learn about you?
- What would you do differently?
- What will be the important issues at the next meeting?
- How did you feel making this call?
- How do you think the prospect felt?
- On a scale of one to five, how would you rate yourself on this call?

Debriefing is a learning experience both for you and for the sales rep. Also, debriefing is an important exercise for you, on your performances.

After I present a seminar, when I come back to my office, I debrief myself using my own preprinted checklist. While we all toss around in our minds what just transpired, use of a checklist forces us to ask ourselves some penetrating questions we might otherwise overlook.

Here are some of the items on my debriefing checklist:

- What stories did I tell?
- What did I learn from my audience?
- What new items do I want to research?
- What will my follow-up be with this client?
- How did I rate on a scale from 1 to 5? What was my strength today?
- What would I do differently?

I don't ask myself what I did wrong or where I was weak. I don't want to give myself an unconscious suggestion of failure. If I am not circling a "4" or "5" for my overall rating I want to know why. If I circle a 5, I want to relive the experience because it felt terrific, and I want to remember what I said or did so I can repeat it.

Similarly, you can create *your own form to help your followers to debrief.* The better you get at debriefing them, the more effective they will be on the job. This process need not be reserved for sales staff. It can be used with anyone you lead who has contact with the customer or client, including tele-marketers or over-the-counter service representatives.

COACHING FOLLOWING A POOR PERFORMANCE

Suppose you accompany a member of the sales team who does an inadequate job. You're sitting there the whole time thinking, "Oh brother," and you can't wait to get this person alone so you can begin some instant, remedial sales training and coaching. I suggest resisting that temptation. Here's why: People usually know when they haven't done the job.

The first thing you might do following the sales call is to not say anything. Let the other person open up. Invariably he or she begins by saying something along the lines, "I don't think I handled that well." Or he might offer you some other entree. If he remains silent, or if nothing happens, I suggest saying, "How do you think you did?" That opens up the conversation—the sales rep is likely to say, "Well, I think I . . ."

You want to learn about the sales rep's perception. You want to know specifically what he thinks he did well, and what he would do differently next time. These questions will suffice. You don't have to ask, "What did you do wrong?" That kind of question connotes failure, and you never want to give an-other the perception that you think he failed.

If the sales rep responds, "I could have done ABC better," your comeback is, "Specifically, how do you think you could have done it better?" Here are a few additional questions that you could pose at this juncture:

- What are you pleased with about your performance?
- What steps will you take next time?
- What follow-up will you make with this prospect?
- Did you learn anything today that you will use on the next call?

Give the sales rep an opportunity to express what he thinks he did right on the sales call. This enables him to reinforce the positive aspects of his presentation. He might say, "I let the prospect do most of the talking." You could then say, ". . . and you feel good about that . . ." and let the sales rep keep talking. At the same time that you are offering this type of listening and coaching to the sales rep, you are also modeling aspects of behavior that you would like the sales rep to emulate when interacting with prospects. Eventually that person will be a better sales rep and may even become a sales manager.

ACKNOWLEDGMENT IS
PART OF COACHING

The best sales coaches offer immediate acknowledgment of the sales rep's efforts. The acknowledgment is reflected in phrases such as:

- When you explained the DEF, the prospect's face really brightened.
- You handled the price objection skillfully.
- You let the prospect do most of the talking and were able to gather a great deal of information.

- Your preparation and planning for this call was very evident.
- You didn't over-promise.

Any experienced sales manager who accompanies a sales rep is going to have a car-load of observations and criticisms regarding the sales rep's performance. Invariably, the sales manager will think of things that could have been said but weren't. During the sales debriefing, she can overwhelm the sales rep with observations, instructions, and criticisms. This is, however, to no avail.

The sales rep is apt to feel like a failure and that her quest to be successful in this profession or organization is hopeless. "I am never going to be able to learn this." "How am I ever going to make a decent income." "I can't please this lady no matter what I do." This is where sales reps begin negative self-talk, and eventually convince themselves that they can't be effective. Conversely, when you listen, ask for permission to make suggestions, offer acknowledgment, and keep steering sales reps to find their own solutions, *you develop the kind of followers who reach their potential.*

"Ellen, specifically, what would you like to do differently on the next sales call as a result of this experience?"

"Margaret, I'm going to maintain unwavering enthusiasm despite the cues I get from the prospect, because I know that our service is going to help them. If he doesn't see it at first, it is not going to diminish my enthusiasm for what we can do for them. Also, for two minutes before I get out of the car, or when I am sitting in the reception area before I see the prospect, I am going to visualize the prospect happily using our services. I am going to qualify my high enthusiasm for what we can do. And we can do great things. That is why I am selling this service."

COACHING, ON THE SPOT

The essence of effective coaching is to be present to the follower and offer the coaching *as it is needed*, at the first appropriate opportunity. The best coaches don't wait until they get back to the office, they know that good coaching happens on the spot. When the sales rep comes up with something he wants to improve upon and ways in which he wants to grow, the sales coach affirms him.

Suppose the sales rep says, "Here are two things I would like to improve on," but you saw some blatant shortcomings in his presentation which he didn't mention. You could then say, "Bob, you know I appreciate you mentioning those things because you were able to identify some things I didn't even see. I am curious to know, however, how do you think you did with XYZ?" You are introducing the opportunity for the sales rep to address what you observed as a flaw. If he still doesn't pick up on it, ask another question.

Suppose that the shortcoming was in the area of planning for the sales call. Your question would be, "Bob, tell me how important do you think planning is for the sales call?" Other questions to pose include:

- "Is it true that planning the sales call can make a difference with what happens during the call?"
- "Can planning time be used to figure out what questions you will ask?"
- "How much time do you think needs to be allocated for planning this call?"

As a result of these questions, the sales rep gets the message that, "yes," planning for the sales call is very important and something that the coach values.

Your next move would be to ask, "How do you think you did in terms of planning for this call?"

Rep: "To tell you the truth, I really didn't spend much time in preparation."

You: "What did that result in?"

Rep: "I was trying to guess the prospect's needs, which comes up frequently on sales call, but I had even less of a clue here because I hadn't spent time before the call. Also, I didn't have the sequence down pat of what I wanted to cover, so my presentation meandered a bit. I might have come off as a little unorganized in the eyes of the prospect."

You: "What would you like to do differently next time?"

Rep: "I would like to spend a little more time before each sales call, but I am afraid that might lead to far fewer sales calls."

Once you have steered the conversation toward the need for preparation, you could say to the sales rep, "Bob, if I'm hearing you correctly you are saying that you're concerned about your use of time, but that you believe it would be beneficial for you to spend more time in the planning process." To reinforce the importance of planning you might review with the rep all of the benefits. They would include:

- Feeling more confident.
- Being more composed.
- Being better organized.
- Asking better questions.
- Creating a better relationship with the prospect.
- Having the client perceive me as brighter, smarter, better.
- Closing sales more quickly and easily.

Suppose the rep is still concerned about how much time preparation requires?

You: "I can understand why you might feel that way. Would you say that the benefit of some preparation in dealing with the prospect once you're face to face with him would outweigh the amount of time necessary for planning? How much time to do you think your precall preparation would take?"

Rep: "You know, I have never actually timed it. It's probably a lot less time than my off-the-cuff perception of it."

You: "How much time would you actually be willing to commit before calling on prospects? In fact, let's take this particular prospect. How much time would you be willing to devote to this prospect before calling on him next time?"

Rep: "I think the average call has been about 15 to 18 minutes. If I walk through the sequence in my mind that will only take about 3 to 4 minutes. Then reviewing notes from the previous encounter and jotting down anything else I want to add would bring the entire time up to about 7 to 8 minutes."

Here you could help the sales rep by pointing out why it may take more or less depending upon your knowledge of the situation. If the rep is making a first call, then he may want to read the annual report, press releases and clippings, or any other information on the prospect. Preparation for the first call could easily exceed 30 minutes or more. A follow-up call, particularly the third or beyond, may take far less time. You've cleared a hurdle when you've got the sales rep *thinking* about planning and building it into his overall sales effort.

GAINING COMMITMENT

A greater goal is for you to get the sales rep to commit to preparation as a necessary and ongoing component of effective selling. By now you may have concluded that this coaching business seems to require a lot of energy and time. "Isn't there any other way to accomplish the same ends?" I've been in enough sales organizations to know that there are few, if any, shortcuts here. Yes, it takes time to enable sales reps to see for themselves the importance of planning the sales call. You have to take them from *awareness to accountability.*

"Bob, it sounds as if you're in agreement that some preparation would make a difference in your calls. What are you willing to commit to today regarding preparation on future sales calls?"

"I am willing to give each call some preparation even though the time may vary widely."

"I think that's wise. How would I know that this is working for you?"

After listening to what the rep has to say, you could also suggest setting up a system of weekly reviews where the rep describes some of the preparation techniques he undertook. Or you might suggest some type of chart. You don't want to make the decision for the sales rep; rather, you want to get him to offer some system for indicating his accountability. He is making a commitment, a promise, and now both of you are merely establishing a simple but effective procedure for helping the rep to be accountable for his promise.

The sales rep might suggest putting a posted pad on the outside of the folder that contains a small checklist that reads:

- Reviewed notes
- Mentally rehearsed presentation
- Visualized the sales call
- Identified in advance some key questions
- Updated notes
- Planned follow-up action

Another system might be to report back on the exception, *i.e.,* tell the sales manager only of those incidents where preparation resulted in extraordinary results. Alternatively, sales reps could report on those times when they failed or neglected to undertake adequate preparation, and what that led to. Optimistically, the failed exception would only represent a few times per week.

Whatever number of suggestions the sales rep may offer, your next step is to say, "What do you think the best system will be to insure that you adequately undertake preparation for each sales call?" You don't really care what the system is, you care about the net effect—*is the sales rep committed to, and accountable for, making adequate preparations on each and every sales call, and is that leading to improved performance?*

You want to have weekly reviews so you can continually support the sales rep, not to use the information to "give him orders." You ask, "How will I know that the system is working?" Once again, the rep will offer his own plan on how you can be easily kept abreast of his progress. The sales rep may suggest that the preparation be added to an internal checklist or he/she may suggest a meeting every Friday at 9 a.m.

As sales manager, surely you can devise a system to ensure accountability, which may generate some resistance. However, *people don't resist their own systems.* When you let them devise and then use their own system to its fullest potential, you get accountability from your followers.

Next you ask, "When will we get this started?" You are apt to hear, "By the end of the week" or by a specific date on the calendar. If this rep's response is by the end of the week, your goal is to get him to say "You mean Friday? At what time?" You want a specific time, to the hour, at which this commitment is initiated.

RANDOM VISITING

As sales coach, periodically you will want to visit customers while not in the company of your sales reps. I regard this as a non-negotiable aspect of your responsibility as a coach and as a leader. The visit is not a sales call. Rather it entails your visiting customers on a scheduled basis and asking "How are we doing in serving you."

Author and consultant Howard Shenson suggests that no matter how many customers your organization serves, it makes sense for you to call all of them periodically just to keep in touch. Shenson suggests that you divide up the alphabet so that you call all your clients beginning with the letters A and B in January, C and D the next month, and so forth. You can combine three in one month when you get down to Q and X. If your organization is not large or you don't have that many clients, you may be able to call clients on a more frequent basis.

We've instituted a plan in our company where every 90 days, if we haven't had contact with a client, we call them. I am personally involved, not just our sales staff. The contact need not be elaborate. You can say "Hi, I just want to reaffirm that we are really glad to be working with you. How can we do an even better job?"

When is the last time you spoke to one of your organization's truck drivers, packagers, telemarketers, or anyone else who has customer contact? And, what will you do as a leader to contribute to their performance with your customers?

Working With Professional and Support Staff

12

*Those who have knowledge should
let others light their candle by it.*
Margaret Fuller

Why have a section on optimizing the performance of professional staff in a book on influencing by design? Because professional staff people are often a breed apart from others in your company and need a special kind of recognition and leadership.

OPTIMIZING THE PERFORMANCE OF YOUR PROFESSIONAL STAFF

My definition of professional staff includes people who:

- Have specific skills.
- Have specific education including at least a college degree, often a Master's degree or beyond.
- Operate in a specific field of endeavor.
- Have continuing education requirements.
- Have industry or professional standards and codes of ethics set for them by governing societies.

Professional staff within your organization could include lawyers, accountants, consultants, architects, programmers, hardware or software specialists, engineers, trainers, writers, and graphic designers, as well as physical therapists, pharmacists, nurses and other health care professionals. Trained to be proficient in specific, technical or clinical skills, they are usually competent in fulfilling their overall job responsibilities.

Earlier, we talked about having functional (I can), adaptive (I am), and technical (I know) types of skills. Professional staff tend to be masters in the third category, technical skills. The challenge working with professional staff is that often their adaptive and functional skills are not as well-developed. As their coach, you can never assume that they have these skills just because they are well paid and otherwise highly proficient in their specific technical areas.

Functional skills call for the ability to lead others, manage others, and manage tasks. They also call for meeting schedules, budgeting, planning, controlling, evaluating, and executing. Adaptive skills, however, are where professional staff are more likely to be deficient. Adaptive skills are the "people" skills—how you relate and interact with others. Adaptive skills are usually not included in the training of professional staff, and often in their early years in the workplace, they received little on-the-job training as well.

The training and education of a professional staff person customarily enable him/her to build relationships with the direct client or customer, *e.g.*, a nurse deals directly with a patient, an accountant works directly with a client. Hence these professionals may not be skilled at serving in the role of team member, seeing the vision, or being a part of the larger organization.

RECOGNIZE THEIR COMPETENCIES

The key to effectively leading professional staff is to recognize their competency and efficiency in their respective fields, even if it is not your field. For example, in the case of a manufacturer, you may be the director of production, but before obtaining such a post you came from the field of administration, not production. Therefore you may be leading others who have skills you do not understand and will never master.

You might come from finance, and now you are supervising the engineers. Without their kind of technical expertise, you could see the situation as disconcerting, but rest your fears: *you do not need to have the specific skills of the people you are leading*. What you need is *an effective relationship with each of your followers so that you know that the work is getting done*, and the competency level and standards and norms are being maintained.

Your continuing goal is to take every opportunity to include professional staff in the overall vision of the organization. This entails looking at where your organization or department, engineering or law firm, consulting or training firm is headed, and where each of your staff fits in.

Make a special effort to meet with them regularly, and much like the coach does in coaching the sales staff. *Debrief them.* Ask them to educate you as to what is going on and what difficulties they are encountering. At the same time, understand that these people need their space and autonomy to work independently within their own professional expertise. Continually define with them their role on the team and their contribution to the organization. Communication, with an emphasis on asking questions and receiving feedback, is critical.

A CASE HISTORY—AN EFFECTIVE
DATA PROCESSING PROFESSIONAL

The following case demonstrates how to successfully lead a professional staff person even when you have no background whatsoever in the functions of that staff person.

Anthony Dickson (names disguised) was hired by a Tulsa, Oklahoma, based civil engineering firm to develop a project tracking system and improve the firm's use of computer graphics. Neil Pierson was Anthony's supervisor. Neil had no background in using data processing equipment and realized that he'd have to heavily rely on Anthony in this area.

Anthony, however, was not like most of the other firm's employees. He seemed aloof and distant, more interested in working on the terminal than interacting with others. Anthony seemed to be marching to the beat of a different drum and sometimes appeared to be lost in space staring at his monitor.

While Neil had solid experience leading in tough situations, Anthony posed a new problem. Neil had little idea how long specific computer-related tasks normally take and thus, how to best monitor Anthony's activities.

Neil determined that he had to take several steps to both effectively serve as leader to Anthony and ensure that a team-like atmosphere and normal supervisory functions were maintained. He set about to find the answers to the following questions, not just for the sake of leading Anthony, but for any time in his career when the situation reoccurred:

- How could he best lead someone when he had no technical background in the professional's discipline?
- What can you look for in an effective data processing professional, and in any type of professional?
- What specific steps are available to ensure that the professional is an active part of the team?
- How can you spot an ineffective professional?

STILL A PART OF THE TEAM

Neil resolved that in working with Anthony he would lead in the same way that he did with his other staff members. So, Anthony was responsible for attending and participating in all staff meetings just like everyone else. This helped to prevent Anthony from becoming isolated from the rest of the project team or developing the notion that the equipment he worked with was more important than his peers or his company.

Reporting and Monitoring—Neil recalled an earlier employee with EDP responsibilities who maintained a closed, almost secretive approach to handling tasks. Neil knew that loyalty comes from being part of a team and that a non-communicative employee or one that maintained privileged information—a corner on the market—was not conducive to an open, cooperative atmosphere.

So Neil prepared specific goals and objectives in consultation with Anthony. He drew up a task list and timetable and met with Anthony daily to review problems encountered and overall progress. At first, Anthony resented these daily meetings, but soon actually began to look forward to them because of Neil's ability to listen to him and to ask the right questions.

To increase Anthony's understanding of the company's ongoing projects, Neil familiarized Anthony with the current forms and controls in use and illustrated how information was handled and compiled. He also took Anthony out to the field so that Anthony could view first-hand what was being accomplished and how his job supported company operations.

Assessing Anthony's Work—Neil realized that no matter how much he learned about EDP and computer graphics, it would take him a long time to be able to evaluate the effectiveness of Anthony's efforts. So Neil set up procedures where he could quickly gain the information he needed regarding Anthony's performance. Neil requested that all programs developed be accompanied by documentation and plain English narrative which explained the importance of each program element. Neil also established a peer review system where Anthony's work was examined by others having familiarity in this area.

Profiling an Effective Professional—Neil read and scanned several data processing magazines, talked with other professionals, got input from Anthony and was able to produce a profile of an effective data processing professional. This was a person who:

- Frequently asks "When do you need to have it?"
- Consistently meets goals.
- Relies on systems manuals—no one on planet Earth can memorize every nuance of every instruction of software and other data processing systems support materials. Successful professionals use the manuals.
- Employs standardized modular/component programs when available. This means no re-inventing the wheel or developing customized programs when adequate programs exist.
- Relies on programming dictionaries.
- Is sharp and articulate just like other competent employees.
- Avoids using computer jargon in explaining what's being done or what has to be done.

DETECTING A POOR PERFORMER

Some EDP professionals cloak their ineffectiveness by inaccurately or inappropriately conveying "hardware" shortcomings. The shortcomings, more often than not, are in their own capabilities. The poor performer may be using dated procedures while machine capability, software, and support systems have increased.

The employee who says, "This can't be done," may really be saying, "I don't know how to do this," or, "My background is insufficient to accomplish the task." The data processing professional who says, "response time will suffer" is often giving a lame excuse. The more appropriate statement may well be, "This will require three-to-five second search delays"—hardly worth canning a necessary function.

One final clue to the poor performing professional is continuing to miss self-determined target dates. If the professional says that project XYZ can be accomplished in six working days, you offer eight days, and it's still not done by the tenth day, few excuses can justify this prolonged execution time.

Neil found no magic or mystery to working with a "computer type" of professional. The time required to accomplish tasks requiring high doses of creativity and innovation can be estimated, similar to non-DP tasks.

A good perspective from which to view the data processing function is that data processing equipment, software, and systems support materials are there to serve the business of your organization and ultimately, human needs.

LEADING OTHER PROFESSIONALS

Independent of who you are leading and what their technical skills are, you can always ask, "How long does that take?" and then ask others in that same field the same question. You can always establish a reporting and debriefing procedure. As the weeks go by you will find yourself becoming more adept at talking their language and beginning to understand exactly what they do and what it means. You can subscribe to a few of their industry journals to keep abreast of the latest trends.

Soon enough, you'll be able to develop yardsticks and benchmarks that let you know the performance level of your professional staff person on a continuing basis. If you use the leadership skills for influencing by design as outlined in previous chapters, and as discussed when coaching a sales staff, you'll find that even a maverick professional staff person will come to respect your leadership capabilities and that you can have an effective relationship.

Here's a checklist for effectively leading any professional:

- Require that professionals report to you regularly with specific information, results and ongoing plans.
- Familiarize professionals with the organization's other projects to help them feel a part of the team.
- Assess their work. Get others' input if you need to.
- Require that projects and programs developed be accompanied by specific documentation.
- Encourage and support participation in professional organizations. These people need peer interaction.
- Provide recognition as you would in leading other staff.

THE SUPPORT STAFF AS PART OF THE TEAM

When leaders think of a team in the business sense, they often think of themselves with their supervisory, professional or sales staff. Administrative assistants, secretaries, clerical workers and other support staff often are not considered part of the team. As a result, many leaders tend to waste the time and talents of the person in the office who could become their most valuable asset.

A top executive quoted in Stephanie Winston's book *The Organized Executive* states, "The best thing that ever happened to me was having a secretary who wanted to work for a company president. I was not the president, so she set out to help me make it. She had a tremendous impact on my effectiveness. And yes, I made it."

To build a winning team with a support staff of two or even 20 requires four progressive steps:

- establishing goals
- considering relationships
- identifying roles
- establishing procedures

First, as with any objective, **goals** need to be established. Both the leader and the support staff need to understand and accept where they are going and how they will get there—as a unit. After goals are established, a team has a tendency to plunge into the "how to's," but there are a few other areas to address first.

The second point in developing a strong team is to **consider relationships.** People who trust and respect one another usually work together more effectively than people who don't. This takes active communication.

The next step is **identifying roles.** Both the leader and follower are aided in knowing what the other person wants, needs, and expects. Ambiguity in who's to do what produces stress and decreases performance.

The last step is **establishing procedures.** These are the methods used to accomplish the team goals and refer to such areas as decision making, problem solving and time utilization.

The winning leader and support staff are considered a partnership. *All share equal responsibility for attaining the success of their team goals.* All need to continually work on active listening, observing each other, reading the non-verbal signals, and telling each other what they think and believe and need.

OTHER CRITICAL FACTORS

It may or may not help to talk to a peer about a problem with one of your support staff. Why not tell the person directly what you would like done and the end results that you need? **Communication** is risky and even uncomfortable, but it can prevent problems.

Being organized is crucial to building a strong team. The leader and support staff need to meet at the end of each day and the end of each week to review their progress and to establish new plans. Use a "to do" list, set priorities, and coordinate your plans. Group questions, comments, and assignments together, and meet for discussion at designated times.

Timing is another critical element. It is best for both leader and support staff to wait for appropriate moments to approach one another. Don't ask for a favor when it's obvious the other person is upset about something. Be considerate of each other's feelings. Courtesy and common sense go a long way in any relationship.

Another critical element is **forgiveness.** To be forgiven, first be forgiving and don't carry grudges. Apologize when you are wrong, too. Learn to lose a battle to win the war. Know which issues are worth fighting for and which are best ignored.

MANAGERIAL CONSIDERATIONS

A professional leader needs to be aware of issues that secretaries themselves most often cite as essential for a superior professional relationship. Below are ten areas of concern to most secretaries. To make your support staff part of a viable, winning team, you have some special responsibilities:

- Treat your secretary as a valued person and vital team member. She/he is a professional in her/his own field. Include your secretary in the office operations and decisions as much as possible. Continually broaden her/his understanding of what you seek to accomplish.

- Allow your secretary the freedom to improve perform-ance by revising systems or changing priorities. Encour-age creativity; allow that there may be many ways to accomplish something.
- Let others know of your trust and faith in your secretary. For example, ask them to deal directly with your secretary in appropriate circumstances. This also helps save your time.
- Keep your secretary informed. Let her/him know where you are and how you can be reached if necessary.
- Avoid asking your secretary to run personal errands. If you need help in this area, hire a shopping service or hire a college student several hours per week.
- Avoid last-minute rush assignments. Plan ahead as best you can. Who appreciates being assigned major jobs at 4:50 p.m. or being collared to handle a last minute assign-ment just before the weekend?
- Delegate, but not just the ordinary. Delegate special, fun projects as well as routine tasks. Your secretary is prob-ably more capable than you realize and it will free your time as well as build her/his sense of value.
- Periodically take telephone calls yourself if your secre-tary needs uninterrupted time to work on priorities.
- Praise in public. Criticize in private. Remember, the be-havior that gets recognized gets repeated!
- Actively look for ways to make your secretary's job more stimulating and less mundane.

SUPPORT STAFF CONSIDERATIONS

To be a productive team member, a professional member of the support staff in turn needs to be aware of issues which concern most leaders. Many leaders would like to see certain initiatives from support staff. Here are eight points to communicate to these valuable people to help them succeed in their roles. Let them know "I expect you to . . ."

- Manage yourself, including maintaining neatness and professionalism in your appearance, punctuality, good attendance and effective use of time.
- Be aware of appropriate telephone image. Recognize that you represent your leader, department, and company! Answer the phone with a smile in your voice.
- Take responsibility for your actions. Accept blame when in error and graciously accept praise for work well done.
- Don't gossip about anyone, especially the boss!
- Make my job easier. Learn to anticipate and initiate. Take on new tasks without always having to be asked, and follow through without having to be reminded or checked on.
- Protect my privacy.
- Be a problem solver instead of a complainer. When a problem arises, come to me with the facts and suggest a solution.
- Broaden your horizons. Develop a bigger picture as to how you fit into the overall workings of our company. Meet peers from other companies by joining professional organizations. Make yourself and the company visible.

Additionally, leaders need to continually assess what they want from this partnership. Compile a list of tasks you would like to add to or upgrade among your support staff's duties. Use the following "Secretarial Task Analysis" (pages 203–204) as a guide.

After using the chart, one busy leader who was responsible for numerous reports realized she could gain more quiet time for thinking and writing if her secretary handled routine correspondence and attended less important meetings for her.

Don't be afraid to turn the tables. Ask your secretary to develop a list of tasks that she/he is now handling or would like to handle. Use the "Secretarial Task Analysis" again. Then sit down together and compare your lists. Consider the discrepancies between the lists, clarify expectations, and make any necessary compromises. Periodically ask each other what you can do to help your partner to become more productive. Also, tell your partner what she or he can do for you to help you become more productive.

THE MANY BENEFITS

A successful winning team of a leader and secretary or support staff has far-reaching ramifications in any organization. If each of you improves the way you interact, you improve your ability to solve problems. Better problem solving means more efficiency and effectiveness in general. This tends to boost morale and decrease stress, turnover, and operating costs. These improvements not only make the bottom line look good, but they also make your organization look good to your employees, your customers, and the public.

SECRETARIAL TASK ANALYSIS

Task	Does She/He Do It Now	If Not, Should She/He Do It	If So, Should She/He Continue	Rate Level of Importance A, B or C
Mail and Paperwork:				
• Opens and sorts incoming mail	☐	☐	☐	☐
• Collects files pertaining to new correspondence	☐	☐	☐	☐
• Discards junk mail	☐	☐	☐	☐
• Can use dictating machine	☐	☐	☐	☐
• Returns typed letters for signature within a day	☐	☐	☐	☐
• Handles routine inquiries	☐	☐	☐	☐
• Brings to your attention papers requiring action	☐	☐	☐	☐
• Drafts replies for your approval	☐	☐	☐	☐
• Handles much correspondence on own, reporting back to you	☐	☐	☐	☐
• Composes letters from your key ideas	☐	☐	☐	☐
Telephone:				
• Asks all callers for their name and nature of their business	☐	☐	☐	☐
• Collects information you'll need for call-backs	☐	☐	☐	☐
• Makes sure you've returned all of your calls	☐	☐	☐	☐
• Handles many calls on her/his own, or refers callers elsewhere, reporting back to you	☐	☐	☐	☐
• Makes many calls for you	☐	☐	☐	☐
Screening:				
• Screens drop-in visitors, directing them elsewhere or sets up appointments for them	☐	☐	☐	☐
• Protects your private time from interruption	☐	☐	☐	☐
• Deals with many drop-in visitors on own, reporting back to you	☐	☐	☐	☐
• Puts files or relevant documents on your desk before scheduled appointments	☐	☐	☐	☐
• Greets visitors; escorts them to your office	☐	☐	☐	☐
• Calls to remind you of "another task" if guests stay past time	☐	☐	☐	☐

Calendar Work:
- Compares your calendar with hers/his daily   ☐   ☐   ☐   ☐
- Knows where to reach you at all times   ☐   ☐   ☐   ☐
- Makes tentative appointments   ☐   ☐   ☐   ☐
- Makes definite appointments for you and coordinates your schedule   ☐   ☐   ☐   ☐
- Maintains tickler file   ☐   ☐   ☐   ☐

Filing:
- Files at least once a week   ☐   ☐   ☐   ☐
- Keeps records-retention plan   ☐   ☐   ☐   ☐

Reading:
- Marks articles and relevant sections of long reports for you   ☐   ☐   ☐   ☐
- Summarizes main points of articles and reports   ☐   ☐   ☐   ☐

Meetings:
- Sits in to take notes   ☐   ☐   ☐   ☐
- Tracks your assignments and when you're the leader, makes sure others do theirs   ☐   ☐   ☐   ☐
- Attends meetings as your representative   ☐   ☐   ☐   ☐

Office Supervision:
- Keeps track of, and orders, office supplies   ☐   ☐   ☐   ☐
- Arranges equipment servicing   ☐   ☐   ☐   ☐
- Funnels clerical work to less senior personnel or temps   ☐   ☐   ☐   ☐

Other Services:
- Makes travel arrangements   ☐   ☐   ☐   ☐
- Arrange office functions: conferences, luncheons, etc.   ☐   ☐   ☐   ☐
- Monitors time to make sure you follow up on daily tasks   ☐   ☐   ☐   ☐
- Takes on independent projects   ☐   ☐   ☐   ☐

This analysis is to be used jointly by the manager and secretary to determine expectations of tasks and clarify communication between them. Level of importance rating: A = Must Do; B = Should Do; C = Would Be Nice To Do. Adapted from *The Organized Executive*, Stephanie Winston, Author.

Making Change
Work For You

13

*We know what we are, but know
not what we may be.*
Shakespeare, *Hamlet*

As we've discussed throughout this book, the world is changing at an unprecedented rate. Whether it is in our lives or in the workplace, we are all challenged with an uncertain tomorrow. I believe that effective leaders of the 1990s increasingly will become adept at envisioning forthcoming changes necessary and vital to the future of their organizations.

Change in itself is not new, only the rate of change is new today—like it or not, we will experience an increasing rate of change. It is unavoidable, particularly in the workplace. The never-ending challenge for you as a leader is to effectively guide yourself, your organization, and your followers through change.

The success of the change is often heavily dependent upon your sensitivity to the followers who frequently face change by decree. We have seen that the process of change can be difficult, and most people have an inherent reflex to resist it—most people would rather continue doing the same things they have been doing, even if they don't achieve desired outcomes.

From this book, and throughout your own career, you have learned that people will resist change, even if they understand the payoffs involved. Change means deviating from an established pattern. We are all creatures of habit and find comfort in sameness, whether it is with relationships, equipment usage, or our environment in general. Who wants disruption, upheaval, alteration or modification? Even if the benefits are extraordinary, change is tough.

RESISTANCE REARS ITS FAMILIAR HEAD

People resist change because they don't know what the actual results will be or what the consequences of making the change will be. Some people simply fear the unknown, reflected in negative self-talk such as:

- I might fail.
- I might be rejected.
- I am not ready.
- I don't know enough.
- I don't have the energy.
- I am already overwhelmed.
- I don't know how.
- Others may find out that I don't know.
- I am not smart enough.
- I am afraid to express my feelings.
- I may not fit.
- I may be the only one who can't learn it.
- I may embarrass myself.
- I am afraid of getting fired.

A relatively small event such as changing the phone system serves to amply illuminate the resistance that people will offer to change in general. Suppose your organization is converting to a new telephone system. Your people have been informed that the new phone system will be installed throughout the organization, and the old phone system will be removed completely.

You anticipate a problem. Your people will probably resist the new phone system much like they resisted the introduction of personal computers a couple years ago in favor of retaining typewriters. The change will begin next week. Here are some verbal and nonverbal clues that employees are resisting acceptance of the new system:

NONVERBAL CUES TO
RESISTANCE TO CHANGE

- People leaving the room during discussion on the new phone system.
- People arriving late to work.
- Procrastination about why there is no available time to devote to learning the new system.
- Offering excuses.
- Using defensive posture, such as tight facial expression or a blank facial expression which indicates that they are not present to the moment.
- Making assumptions about other people to justify their own resistance, *i.e.*, "No one else is learning it."
- Presenting limited self conceptions: "I'm too old to change." "I'm not smart enough to make this change. It took me so long to learn the last system."
- Citing your lack of appreciation for their situation, "You wouldn't understand," or "You're not the one who has to go through this. You don't have to work with these dumb buttons."
- Expressing beliefs such as, "It will never work," or, "I don't know why they brought this in here; this is a terrible system."
- Blaming others, particularly those who chose this phone system: "I'm not sure Ed knew what he was doing when he bought this system."
- Labeling others, *i.e.*, "Ed is a dummy, there is no way he could have paid good money for this system."

- Denying the need to change. "What was wrong with the old system? It worked fine for me. I just don't see the need to change."

Particularly among older workers, but by no means confined to them, some followers will resist change by exhibiting technophobia. "I am not good at using the digital gadgets." "I am not a technical person." Others may resist for reasons even they cannot articulate; their fear of change may be on a nonconscious level.

Often these concerns are expressed as statements that begin with what if . . . or how about . . . Some resisters envision a scenario in which the change leads to horrendous results, even though they have little evidence to support this conclusion.

These kinds of situations call for a leader who is able both to identify and surface such resistance and to serve as a friendly, well-informed, ever-present resource and sounding board for followers through this challenging period. The key to effectively implementing change is to recognize in advance that resistance will always be a part of the process and that rather than running from it, effective leaders build plans for dealing with resistance into the change process. Moreover, the effective leader becomes skilled at identifying resistance or change.

LASTING CHANGE FOLLOWS A FIVE-STEP PROCESS

Psychologist Brian Hall describes change as a five-step sequential process including:

				Action
			Commitment	
		Acceptance		
	Understanding			
Awareness				

All steps need to be completed before lasting change can occur.

Awareness—This is the primary stage; no change can take place without first having an awareness of the forthcoming change. As a coach or leader who is influencing by design, after you've worked with all five steps of this process more closely, you'll realize that its success is based upon your ability to create the awareness among your followers which will carry them through all of the five phases to achieve the desired outcome.

Understanding—Ian D. Percy, president of the Percy Group in Toronto says, "To effectively create organizational change you must first give people knowledge. Knowledge helps change attitudes and new attitudes can change personal behavior. Change in the personal behavior of individuals, in turn, leads to organizational change."

As leader, you face a yeoman's job in ensuring that all followers have complete understanding of why the changes are necessary. Your people's understanding helps create an environment in which acceptance of the change can take place. It is not enough to simply give your followers information about the change, they need to understand for themselves why the change is necessary. It could be that the prior system doesn't have enough capabilities, will not be adequate with the new department being added, or any of a number of other reasons.

Acceptance—By now, your people are saying, "Okay, we've got the message, we understand why change is being made." On at least an intellectual basis, they offer acceptance. You are, however, only at the second step of five in terms of successfully implementing this change.

Commitment—Next, each of your followers needs to commit to actively support the change, reflected in such affirmations as:

"I will attend the briefing session."
"I will read the manual."
"I will experiment with the phone."

In addition, your staff needs to go further:

"I will attempt multi-step procedures immediately."
"I am free to make errors."
"I am willing to embarrass myself."
"I will take chances."
"I am committed to whatever steps are necessary to effectively master the use of this new telephone system."
"I will support others' effective use of this new system."

Action—Of all the steps, action is the most evident. It is reflected by staff members vigorously working with the new phone system, reading manuals, talking about it, dialing and receiving. When is the change fully implemented? When the new phone system and its capabilities become the in-house standard—nobody is resisting, and nearly everyone is using it effectively.

I don't feel that you can make anyone accept anything. Followers can do the job, but they may not offer the type of acceptance necessary to make the change the type of success you seek. They also have the onus of responsibility for making the commitment and taking the action necessary to be proficient users of the new phone system. From the third stage on, *your role becomes one of primarily answering questions, being available to listen, and serving as a model for behavior.*

ACTION STEPS FOR FACILITATING CHANGE

Some change happens dramatically, rapidly separating a person or organization from how their world was. Other changes happen more gradually allowing for planning and contingencies. A leader's role is to be responsive to change at whatever pace it comes. Her role remains that of helping others to acknowledge and accept *what now is.*

Whether it is changing the phone system, adding or down-sizing a department, merging, expanding or reorganizing, the five steps—awareness, understanding, acceptance, commitment and action—stay the same. So too, the type of resistance you will encounter is fairly predictable. To encourage acceptance of healthy change, you have several alternatives.

Create a vision of the positive effects the change will bring—On a small scale, you can create a new vision for your followers of how things will be once the new system is familiar to them. For instance, with the new phone system, relate to your staff how you will all be better able to serve customers, *i.e.*, you are going to rotating lines, a system where everyone will be able to answer their own calls directly, or there will be fewer lost calls.

Always relate to your followers' *personal bottom lines*—the "what's in it for me," factor. Relate the changes to how, specifically, each will benefit as an individual:

"The new system will offer enhanced accounting accuracy, reduce costs, and potentially increase everyone's annual bonus."

Continually communicate the new vision and new plans through personal meetings and conferences—Often organizations use an annual meeting or conference to explain what changes they will be making and how they are going to get from A to B. Your role is to extend the message in these larger gatherings to small groups and one-on-one settings.

Provide extra support to your team members—your people will need to have you wander by their desks more often, and ask them how things are going. They want your reinforcement and acknowledgment:

"I know this is uncomfortable for you."
"I appreciate what you are going through."
"I can understand that this change is challenging for you."

Acknowledgment helps others to not feel isolated and frustrated, and continues to be one of the most underrated leadership tools available.

Affirm value of others to the organization—Many employees, no matter how long they have been with the organization, see change as fearful because they question whether they will still be needed. Your goal is to affirm their value to the organization and define how their roles are going to change. They need to know SPECIFICALLY how the change is going to affect them.

One of my longterm clients, the GE Answer Center® located in Louisville, had ten supervisory positions. Senior management decided a reorganization was necessary and eliminated the supervisory position. Naturally each supervisor wanted to know "how is this going to affect me? Will I even have a job?" In this case, the supervisor role was re-defined as having two major functions—responsibilities for administrative and personnel issues and development of the staff of phone representatives. And it was decided to have supervisors dedicated to each function.

As a group, senior management and the ten "former" supervisors discussed the changes. A mutual agreement was reached as to which staff members would assume which roles. Then the ten were given guidance on how to make the most of their skills in the new role and to engage in their "best work." Titles were changed to "specialists." Their value to the organization was reinforced specifically and individually. Because senior management thought through and planned the change, and involved the employees directly affected, the change was positively received.

Be a model of flexibility yourself—Be the first one to start using the phone system. It's okay for you to express doubt, *i.e.*, "This is tough for me too, but I accept the value of this change for the organization."

In the movie "The Battle of the Bulge," Robert Shaw plays a German general who takes a declining amount of rations daily to match the rations that his troops receive. As the campaign wears on, each day the troop's rations decrease further. One evening, the general is brought a full plate of dinner which far exceeds anything the troops have seen in weeks. He knocks the plate away in fit of rage telling the server, "I want to know how strong my men are. Bring me the same rations that they get."

Use humor to relieve the stress of change—Look for the lighter side of things. Don't be afraid to laugh with your followers regarding some of the changes going on. Take time to play together. It's an opportunity to share in each other's humanness.

Give your followers the time to talk and ask questions— Many of their fears can be alleviated simply through their ability to express themselves. Make the time to be present to people in a relaxed way so they will want to talk with you.

Be sensitive to their fears—don't lightly dismiss others' fears with statements such as, "It's just a phone, it is not going to bite you." Recognize that though the change may not challenge you, if it's a big deal to some of your followers, then it's a big deal. If you try to downplay or minimize it, you will be far less effective with them than if you remain sensitive to their concerns.

Allow sufficient time for change to occur—Adoption of new ways of doing things usually occurs at a slower rate than most leaders would prefer. Be patient. To move from awareness to action takes some people longer than others. You may have had two weeks lead time to become familiar with the new system, your followers may need more. In massive organizational change, the transition phases are months and years.

Get people involved in creative ways to deal with change— Ask your staff, "How can we as a unit more effectively deal with this change?" Hold a brainstorming session if necessary. Solicit all inputs. Solutions could include everyone offering one item they've learned about the new system, people teaming up with each other, each person being responsible for selected portions of the user manual, team members role playing with each other, or other approaches.

LEARNING BY UNLEARNING

To help people learn new ways of doing things, often you have to help them *unlearn*—to assess what they are doing now and acknowledge that it is not going to be effective or appropriate based on the direction the organization or team is taking. "But the typewriter is working fine, why do I have to change to a word processor?" The organization and the individual may no longer be competitive if they stay with the old system.

How do you help someone unlearn? Everything starts with awareness. Help people to understand why they have been doing what they have been doing and the results it has enabled them to generate. Keep taking small steps until the uncomfortable begins to become somewhat comfortable.

Influencing your staff by design in the face of change requires continually acknowledging their efforts, and reinforcing why the change better supports the mission of the organization or department. Viewed in this context, *acknowledgment and reinforcement are just as important as any technical training program.*

HOW DO YOU VIEW CHANGE?

Many of the major growth periods in our lives and in our organizations come as a result of change. As Vivian Buchen says in her book, *Welcome Change*, "One change makes way for the next giving us the opportunity to grow." Sheila Murray Bethel, in *Making a Difference: 12 Qualities that Make You a Leader*, says, "By serving your people as a change master and by trying to help them learn to change, you will be making a difference."

The way that we view change is reflected in our attitudes. Attitudes are the way we think. We may not always have control over a situation, but we always have control over our attitudes. Here's how to maintain a healthy attitude toward change:

Look on the light side—Hold the change in your mind as part of growing. Whether it is one of your followers continually coming in for guidance or another lamenting that he or she will never learn the new system, be a light touch. Without denigrating the system itself, or giving your followers reason to do so, make light of the changes when possible.

Find a friend you can talk with—Whether you are a leader or a follower, the ability to express yourself to another helps make any change become more tolerable.

Find a friend you can cry with—Likewise, if something is very upsetting to you, commiserate with another. You will instantly feel better and whatever was upsetting you will not loom as large. Give yourself permission to show emotion or even cry, as it is often just the catharsis you need.

Read an uplifting book—Read about others who have effectively handled great changes. Or simply read a book that has a motivational or inspirational focus. For example if you have been reading Profiles in Courage, you might be less hesitant to gripe about changes in the telephone system.

Listen to an inspirational cassette tape—This provides the same benefit as a book. You can even sleep while listening and your subconscious mind will absorb the message. Use cassette tapes during commuting time.

Keep a journal—Writing crystallizes thought. A journal is an effective way for you to express your fears, frustrations, doubts and concerns. Writing how you feel, much like speaking with another, is an effective outlet for expression. Once you see your fears and concerns written on paper, often they don't loom as large.

Sing a song—Literally. If you are in the shower, or walking down the sidewalk, express yourself through music; as an alternative, play some uplifting music. Don't laugh, but the theme song from "Rocky," or "Chariots of Fire," can work wonders.

Identify your fears as accurately as possible—Ask yourself what you are really afraid of. Be honest as to whether the fears are well-founded or only False Expectations Appearing Real (FEAR).

Look for new learning—Consider the learning opportunities that the change presents. Will you be more proficient with the new equipment and hence a more productive person? Will you become more responsive when learning to use other types of equipment? Will you become a more valuable manager? Ask for what you need—whether it is support, additional instruction, or a break in the action, ask for what you need. Don't be a silent sufferer; no one is handing out any medals.

Use affirmations—In Chapter 4 we discussed the power of saying or thinking simple statements that reflect desired outcomes. I suggest you create affirmations regarding changes which you presently face. "I can handle this," is a simple affirmation that works well for me. You can insert the word "easily" to create the affirmation, "I can easily handle this."

There is not a whole lot you can't handle, and we are all stronger and better-equipped than we often give ourselves credit for. *Conversely if you tell yourself, "I can't handle this," "I am not going to be able to make it," or, "This is so difficult," then you'll probably be right. Negative self-talk reinforces negative results.*

Take extra care of your body—Change is usually a time of stress and so it is not the time to shortchange rest, nutrition, or other types of physical support. When your body is under stress it is affected in many different ways. Your digestive system may not work as well. Your heart rate and blood pressure may vary. Treat yourself during this period to an extra work out, massage, or whatever helps you take more effective care of your body.

Facing Change and the Challenge of Leadership, Head On—After all is said and done, sometimes the only approach to change that will work is plunging in and facing your fear, which is always temporary. Since influencing by design is best accomplished through modeling the behavior you seek in others, facing your fears head on may be the most powerful signal you can offer. Once you get started, a new set of challenges may arise, but fear is no longer one of them.

EFFECTIVE LEADERSHIP IS NO ACCIDENT

As we've seen throughout this book, effective leadership is not a matter of luck. You exert influence on your followers or employees every minute of every day. When you become proficient at influencing by design, the people who look to you for guidance, support, and behavioral cues, have a far better chance of being successful.

Whether your staff numbers one or one thousand, by enthusiastically and continually expanding your level of awareness and recognition of how your attitudes, beliefs, activities, and appearance influence your followers, you have touched the heart of leadership. It's no accident; you are increasing your ability to influence by design.

> *What we call the beginning is often*
> *the end, and to make an end is*
> *to make a beginning. The end is*
> *where we start from.*
>
> T.S. Eliot

Bibliography

Books

Albrecht, Karl, Ph.D., *At America's Service*. Homewood, IL: Dow Jones-Irwin, 1988.

Bethel, Sheila Murray, *Making A Difference: 12 Qualities to Make You a Leader*. New York: G.P. Putnam, 1990.

Beveridge, Don Jr., and Jeffrey P. Davidson, *The Achievement Challenge: How to be a 10 in Business*. Homewood, IL: Dow Jones-Irwin, 1988.

Blanchard, Kenneth and Norman Vincent Peale, *The Power of Ethical Management*. New York: William Morrow, 1988.

Block, Peter, *The Empowered Manager*. San Francisco: Jossey-Bass, 1988.

Burley-Allen, Madelyn, *Listening*. New York: Wiley, 1982.

Conklin, Dr. Robert, *How to Get People to Do Things*. Chicago: Contemporary Books, 1979.

Covey, Stephen, *The Seven Habits of Highly Effective People*. New York: Simon & Schuster, 1989.

Davidson, Jeffrey, *Blow Your Own Horn: How to Market your Career and Yourself*. New York: AMACOM, 1987.

Eliot, T. S., *Selected Poems*. New York: Harcourt, Brace Jovanovich, 1964.

Fensterheim, Herbert, and Jean Baer, *Don't Say Yes When You Want to Say No*. New York: Dell, 1975.

Frankl, Victor, *Man's Search for Meaning*. New York: Simon & Schuster, 1988.

Gardner, John W., *No Easy Victories*. New York: Harper & Row, 1968.

Garfield, Dr. Charles, *Peak Performance*. New York: Morrow, 1986.

Greenleaf, Robert, *Servant Leadership*. Mahwah, NJ: Paulist Press, 1977.

Half, Robert, *How to Check References When References are Hard to Check*. New York: Robert Half Associates, 1988.

Half, Robert, *Robert Half on Hiring*. New York: Crown, 1985.

Herman, Roger E., *Keeping Good People: Strategies for Solving the Dilemma of the Decade*. Cleveland: Oakhill Press, 1990.

Jacobson, Bernard, *Conductors on Conducting*. New York: Columbia, 1979.

Jeffries, Elizabeth, *Person To Person*. Louisville, The Leadership Press, 1990.

Kelley, Robert, *The Gold-Collar Worker*. Reading, MA: Addison-Wesley, 1985.

Kotter, John, *The Leadership Factor*. New York: Free Press, 1988.

LeBoeuf, Michael, Ph.D., *The Greatest Management Principle in the World*. New York: G.P. Putnam, 1986.

Levering, Robert, *A Great Place to Work*. New York: Random House, 1988.

Maccoby, Michael, *Why Work: Leading the New Generation*. New York: Simon and Schuster, 1988.

Meek, Charles, *Conducting Made Easy*. Metuchen, NJ: Scarecrow Press, 1988.

Powell, John, *Why Am I Afraid to Tell You Who I Am?* Chicago: Argus Communications, 1969.

Winston, Stephanie, *The Organized Executive*. New York; Warner, 1989.

Zemke, Ron, *The Service Edge*. New York: New American Library, 1989.

Zunin, Dr. Leonard and Natalie Zunin, *Contact: The First Four Minutes*. New York: Ballantine, 1986.

Articles

"WordPerfect's Corporate Culture is a Model." *PC Week*, Volume 5, pg. 53, September 26, 1988 by Will Fasti.

Author

Elizabeth Jeffries is a nationally recognized professional speaker, seminar leader, consultant and author who specializes in leadership and change strategies for the 21st century. She is known for her innovative work with leaders, inspiring, encouraging and challenging them to *live and lead from the inside out.*

In 1981, Jeffries set out to help solve people problems in organizations across America. Originally educated in the health care field, she combined her strong orientation to service, her years of experience in leadership and management and her passion for people. Today, Jeffries has addressed over a half million people in more than 2000 presentations. Her clients are hospitals, health systems, professional associations and businesses throughout the United States and Canada.

An active member of the National Speakers Association, she serves on its Board of Directors and is one of a select group of less than 10 % of its membership who has earned the prestigious designation of CSP - Certified Speaking Professional.

The Heart of Leadership: Influencing by Design is Jeffries' second book. Her first book, **Person to Person, Making Connections with Others and Yourself** is a personal leadership handbook. Jeffries lives in Louisville, Kentucky.

For information on Elizabeth Jeffries' speeches, seminars, learning materials and newsletter, *The Leadership Letter*, please contact her at:

Jeffries & Associates
P.O. Box 24495
Louisville, KY 40224
502-339-1600 FAX 502-339-1232